## Advance Praise For *Turning Change Into A Payday*

"I was once told 'you have the rest of your life to become the person you REALLY want to be, or to DEFEND the person you are.' *Turning Change Into A Payday* represents a how-to approach that goes beyond catch-phrases and includes the reader in a thoughtful exploration of how to overcome the barriers – mostly self-imposed – to practical, positive change in our lives."
- Joshua D. Williams, VP Seattle Business Banking Group, Wells Fargo Bank, N.A.

"This is a must read book for people confronting change in business or life. Ralph Bruksos leads us through the eight stages of change and shows us how we can positively influence the outcome."
- H. James Fitzgerald, President, Weyerhaeuser Asia (Retired)

"I've read numerous books on change. This one is different, because Bruksos writes from the heart. He walks his talk. As he tells many of his directly experienced heart-warming stories about people who have overcome huge bariers to succeed, he instructs us about how we can grow, change, and succeed in our lives. In chapter two, for example, the author dramatically illustrates how he personally overcame great odds, changed and succeeded. It's one of the best chapters I have ever read about one man's marathon to victory."
-Gary A. D'Angelo, Ph.D., President, D'Angelo & Associates

To Staci
Warmly,
Ralph Bruksos

Ralph Bruksos
with Paul C. Tumey

# Turning Change into a Payday

## Re-inventing Yourself Through the Eight Stages of Change

Training Consultants        Seattle, Washington

ISBN: 9768566-0-3
First Printing, June 2005

If you want to change, to grow, someone or something will appear in your life to help you.

Possibly, for some, it will be this book.

-Ralph Bruksos

# Acknowledgements

I am indebted to those who influenced me with positive encouragement and helpful suggestions on making this book better. I especially want to thank **Ralph Palmen**; **Gary D'Angelo, PhD**; **Michael Grove**; **Doug Merlino**; **Cassandra Miller**; **Francine Viola**; and **Paul C. Tumey**. Your belief in this book helped make it possible.

# Dedication

When I addressed the 1975 annual meeting of Carrier heating and air conditioning dealers, sponsored by AIREFCO, Inc., **Jerry Rochford** sat in the audience. A Carrier dealer himself, Jerry hired me as a consultant and introduced me to other Carrier dealers, who became my clients. Countless related introductions from Jerry followed. It was Jerry who introduced me to a large public utility that retained me for 25 years. The great success of my career as a consultant and trainer is largely a result of Jerry Rochford's belief in me. In my book I discuss the importance of associating with those who inspire, teach and empathize with us. I am eternally grateful for Jerry's generosity and most of all, his caring. It is with this sense of gratitude that I dedicate this book to Jerry Rochford.

# Table of Contents

# Forward

Ralph Bruksos was the first person to shed the light of truth about selling to me back in 1978, when he so quietly — yet powerfully — pointed out the enormous difference between simply helping people to buy my products, and that of actually committing to helping them succeed. Ralph's teachings altered the course of my life and gave me wealth and happiness beyond my dreams. In this book, Ralph reveals the very same truths that have guided me, and his legions of followers to success beyond any one's imagination.

Ralph Waldo Emerson perhaps said it best when he penned: "The poet brings his poem, the shepherd his lamb, the farmer, corn, the miner, a gem, the sailor, coral and shells, the painter, his picture, the girl, a handkerchief of her own making." So, one might say, the teacher brings his teachings. A gift from Ralph Bruksos could be not more appropriate than this generous collection of his rich wisdom from the depths of his mind and heart.

The messages in this book echo Ralph's sustaining kindness. His immortal truth about who he is and what he has learned illuminates every passage. As you read these words, you will be in the company of a true, wise friend, expert guide and caring coach. I believe you will find yourself, as I did, underlining virtually every page as lights flash on in your mind that here, at last, are the words of an authentic master of change.

I am sure that the person who reads these pages will be forever changed and permanently indebted for their value.

You are in for a rare and precious treat.

### - Jim Cecil

Author of *The Heart of the Farmer* and founder of Nurture Marketing

# Introduction

### *Finding the good*

I arrived at my Seattle, Washington office at 6:20 a.m. that morning. The phone rang as I was making coffee.

"Have you heard about Ralph?" It was my friend George, calling to tell me that Ralph Palmen, my friend, mentor, and spiritual guide, had been shot in Los Angeles the night before. Ralph Palmen was – and remains – one of the great people in my life, a generous man with an extraordinary sense of humor. He was also an avid golfer, and we played together regularly.

Shocked, I asked George, "Is he still alive?" He said, "I don't know."

I immediately called the hospital and talked to the receptionist. I asked to speak to the nursing station for a patient named Ralph Palmen. To my surprise, instead of a nurse, Ralph answered the phone. Flooded with relief that he was alive, I asked, "What happened?"

In a weak voice, my old friend described how he had gone to Los Angeles the day before to make a presentation. As was his custom when out of town, he went to a baseball game.

On his way back from the game, Ralph parked some distance from the motel lobby. As he was making his way from his rental car across the well-lit parking lot, he noticed a man coming up to him on his left. The man said, "Excuse me, sir. Do you have a minute?" Ralph then looked to see another man closing on his right, who said, "Just a minute, sir. Let me ask you something." Ralph made an instant decision and ran for the lobby of the motel. What he didn't see was a third man behind him who raised a shotgun and fired, hitting Ralph in the back.

Even though he had been shot and wounded, Ralph kept running.

He managed to make it to the motel lobby, where he fell and lay bleeding on the floor. People walked around him, probably assuming he was drunk or high. There is a bit of irony here. Ralph, being the spiritual man he is, was then president of his church board, taught Sunday school, and never drank or used drugs.

After about ten minutes, someone noticed that he was bleeding and called 9-1-1. The medics rushed him to the hospital. He was immediately taken into surgery.

He survived the surgery, came out of the anesthesia, and was lying there in a hospital bed, sorting out the details of his experience, when I called.

He explained to me that he had been contemplating his good fortune: at least he was still alive.

Then he said words that have resonated with me ever since: "You know, in all of our years together, you and I have always tried to find the good in everything that has happened to us. After thinking about it for three hours in somewhat of a haze, I finally figured out that this is probably going to slow down my back swing and improve my game."

I was impressed and grateful for his incredible attitude. Even with this traumatic near-death experience, undergoing surgery, being alone in a distant city, he was still looking for the good.

When change happens, if that change is inevitable, we must find a way to accept it.

Ralph's prediction was on the money. His injury has slowed down his back swing and his golf game has improved. He has also continued to forge a marvelously successful career as speaker, author, business executive and spiritual leader.

What Ralph did for himself is what I wrote this book to help others learn to do. When change happens, traumatic or not, we can find the good, study it, experience it, and — believe or not — we can be grateful for the experience. Whatever happens, our lives can be enriched by *any* change, if we search for the good in it.

An important part of mastering change is "finding the silver lining." This is not easy. It requires courage, discipline and self-knowledge.

Most of us are taught to fear change at an early age, and this fear stays with us as long as we allow it to. This book will help you free yourself from that fear by helping you better understand what change is, how it works, and how to master it.

**If you understand the concept of change, you will not fear it, no matter what shape it takes.**

### *Understanding change: what it will do for you*

This book aims to help you view change as an opportunity, to turn it into a payday. By "payday," I don't mean only monetary rewards, although managing change effectively can certainly be good for the bottom line. At the same time, change can lead you to learn new skills, to improve your fitness, to open yourself to new experiences, or to become closer to your loved ones. I've learned that the rewards of mastering change usually benefit both your financial *and* emotional health.

Change comes in many forms. It can arrive in the form of a shift in management at your workplace, an unexpected layoff, an injury, a death in the family, or a change in a close relationship. Much in our lives often seems uncertain: we live with volatility in the stock market, the economy, even the threat of terrorism. Change itself seems to happen faster and faster.

Change can also come at our own instigation, when we decide to take charge and make a positive transformation. When we decide to improve our relationships, continue our educations, to set our goals high, to face our fears and commit ourselves to growth.

Over the last four decades, I've worked with an incredibly diverse array of people and businesses – from small companies to large corporations – and tried to help give them the tools to manage change successfully. It has been a privilege and a fantastic educational experience. This book presents the core of what I have learned.

I began to formally study change in 1960, after two friends each sent me a copy of the same article from the *Harvard Business Review* ("Marketing Myopia," by Ted Levitt, July-August 1960).

The article examined the impact of change on the railroad industry. Surprisingly, it said the reason that the railroads were going bankrupt was not because of competition from long-haul trucks and other means of transportation, but because they had failed to see the challenges to their prosperity and *change accordingly.*

At the time, I was the executive vice president and chief operating officer of a firm with twenty-three branches in the United States and Canada. I was also a speaker and consultant on the then very popular discipline of time management. I had trained thousands of people in top companies and even produced a vinyl record (remember those?) on the subject.

Soon after I received the *Harvard Business Review* article from my friends, I read about a fishing boat disaster in Alaska and the boat's amazingly resilient captain. Something clicked. As involved as I was in time management, I had found a new love. I began a life-long journey of discovery on the topic of "change."

But change is not just something I study.

In fact, often more than I would wish, it has been a way of life. The path I've traveled to where I am today has taken more than enough turns to induce whiplash.

I have been incarcerated, the president of a nationwide company, a millionaire, and later so broke I had to borrow money from my teenage daughter. Well into my forties, with a family to support, I had to rebuild a successful career from the ground up.

As I've worked to help my clients, I've also battled the unexpected twists in my own life. All of the information in this book is informed by those struggles.

I've done many things in order to cope with my own demons. To combat a fear of heights, I have parachuted from a plane and climbed mountains. To test my endurance, I began to run marathons when I was almost fifty.

I've come to believe that the only way to effectively deal with change is to view it as an opportunity. The techniques described in this book will help you do that. They will help you recognize change and learn to meet it head on. They will help you cope with difficult times. They will help you learn to *turn change into a payday*.

### *From "change victim" to "change master"*

I've observed that people deal with change in one of three ways:

1.  Some people barely cope. They are always off balance. They resist, complain and cast blame. These are change *victims*.

2.  Others get their lives back to normal after awhile and return to the way life was before the change occurred. They plod along. Regardless of what happens – even trauma – they put one foot in front of the other and

17

continue to trudge forward. These are change *neutrals*.

3. Then there are those who use the experience of change to form a band of steel down their backbones, to give them a "Ph.D." in life. They never seem to have bad luck. They learn, grow and achieve their goals because, to them, change is an opportunity. These are change *masters*.

When you have learned how to recognize and adapt to change – even change that happens so quickly and dramatically you are unable to prepare for it – you become a "change master." You accept change and convert it into something positive. You find a way to make it have a personal payday. This book will help you get to that point.

## *The eight stages of change*

Change is a complex process, and everyone reacts to differently, at their own individual pace.

I've noticed that people tend to experience change in eight stages. While this process is by no means ironclad, most people seem to go through some version of each of these stages.

This book is organized along the lines of these eight stages, with a chapter devoted to each. As you read each section, it might help think about your experiences of change and how they relate to each stage.

Before we begin an in-depth discussion of each step, let me summarize them here.

## Stage One: Hypothermia

In this stage, we are unaware that change is coming and will deny it is necessary. In fact, some experience a mild euphoria, even though they may be frozen in important parts of their lives.

## Stage Two: Discomfort

As we either gradually "thaw out" or are shocked out of our complacent mindset with a traumatic event, we begin to intuit that something doesn't feel right.

This feeling of discomfort or restlessness can occur in any area of our lives: our relationships, our financial situations, our environments, or our careers. Some ignore the signals of discomfort and as the years go by, they become increasingly unhappy. They work hard to block out uneasiness and allot more and more resources to maintaining the "status quo."

At some point, something occurs that pushes us to the next stage.

## Stage Three: Analysis

In this stage, we begin a careful examination of the situation. The idea that a change might be happening is considered. This stage is filled with questions. "What's going on?" "Why do things feel different?" "What's making me uncomfortable?"

There is also a great deal of resistance in this stage, usually motivated by the need to feel that we are right and others are to blame.

## Stage Four: Exploring

In the fourth stage, we begin to explore other possibilities and the consequences of each. "What would it be like if we moved?" "Would I be happier if I made less money but worked at a job I loved?" "How would I feel if I were married instead of single?" "Now that my mother has died, how would it feel if we were to sell her house?" "How stressful would it be if I started my own business?"

At stage four, we might seek a role model who has gone through a similar change and is enjoying a happier life. In this stage, alternatives are visualized and contemplated, signaling a deeper acceptance of the change that has already begun.

## Stage Five: Experimenting

In this stage, the alternatives we contemplated are tested in various ways. When we reach this stage, we are completely thawed out and our icy reluctance to change is replaced by an increasing desire to "get on with it." Still, because we are unsure of where we heading, we will go through a period of testing. Some couples choose to live together before they commit to marriage. People like to test-drive a car before they buy it. Someone might visit the foreign city in which they have a new job offer to see how it feels. While experimenting, we have a great opportunity to learn from others. The greater someone fears a change, the longer this period tends to be. The experimental stage is a sign that change is around the corner.

## Stage Six: Decision

By stage six, a definite change has occurred. A decision has been made and acted upon. To reach this stage, significant fears may have been overcome.

## Stage Seven: Commitment

This stage is about maintaining the gains we have already achieved. When we make a change, we sometimes push back against it and try to figure out ways to revert back to the way we were. This resistance is often subconscious. If we are able to persist, then the change takes root in our lives… and blossoms. This is the stage at which we can choose to make excuses — what I call "getting our story straight" — or to "close the loop" and finalize the change.

## Stage Eight: Recycling

This can occur at any point in the process. It is natural to recycle through some of the stages. Many of our journeys through change chart a complex course where we might go through **Discomfort**, **Analysis** and **Exploring** only to lapse back into **Discomfort** for a time.

Just as our bodies might reject an organ transplant, our lives might reject a change. This is our way of coping. Some may call this stage a relapse, but it is actually a valuable and necessary – if exasperating – stage of change. Also, because nothing stays the same for very long, we can expect that at some point life will call upon us to go through this cycle over and over.

### *Getting started*

Now we're ready to begin our journey. It's my goal to offer help as we go, to be your guide through this daunting process. I have known a great many remarkable people over the years, and I will use examples from their lives, my own life, and the wisdom of others to offer insight about each stage as well as the encouragement to move to the next.

Remember, everyone moves at his or her own pace, so don't be too hard on yourself. By understanding the process, cultivating a sincere desire to always find the good, and realizing that we have tremendous power to channel our energies, we can learn to turn change into a payday.

# Stage One: Hypothermia

In this stage, we are unaware that change is coming and will deny it that is necessary. In fact, some experience a mild euphoria, even though they may be frozen in important parts of their lives.

### *Hypothermia: when everything is "just fine"*

Years ago, I read an incredible story about a crab boat fishing in Alaska that led me to a new way of thinking about the process of change, specifically when we are "frozen."

It was a cold January evening in Kodiak. The boat was loaded with crab and safely tied up. It was snowing, and a strong wind was blowing across the bay.

At around 8:00 p.m., the captain decided to go over to a cannery pier a few miles away, perhaps to be the first in line to unload in the morning. Along with his two crewmen, the captain untied the boat and headed out into the open water. With the darkness, the wind and the snow, visibility was very limited. As they were entering the little cove where the cannery was located, they hit a rock.

The captain realized the seriousness of the situation and hailed the U.S. Coast Guard in Kodiak on the boat's radio. After sounding, "Mayday! Mayday!" he gave their exact location and described what had happened. Unfortunately, in the chaos of the moment, it was unclear to him whether the Coast Guard had received the transmission.

Within minutes, the vessel capsized, sending the three men into the dark, freezing water. One crewman, a Yugoslav, did not surface. The captain and remaining

"Hell begins on the day that God grants us a clear vision of all that we might have done, all that we might have accomplished, and that which we did not do."

**Gian-Carlo Menotti**, Italian opera composer who was 93 years old in 2005

crewman swam to the shore, a short distance away, and climbed onto the slippery rocks at the base of a cliff.

They were soaking wet and very, very cold. Their bodies had lost more heat than they could generate and they were slipping into hypothermia. Their breathing slowed, and they felt drowsy. Despite being so cold, they were not shivering and, in fact, they had ceased to feel any discomfort or pain. After a few minutes, the surviving crewman relaxed his grip on the rocks and quietly slipped into the water.

Shortly after, several Coast Guard boats arrived, formed a grid pattern, and began a search. Shining strong searchlights, they crossed and re-crossed the area where the boat had gone down. They found debris from the vessel floating in the icy waters.

During this time, the captain stood on the shoreline watching the Coast Guard's search. The radio speakers on the boats broadcast the searchers' conversation. It was clear to the captain that no one had thought to look along the shoreline.

He considered swimming the few hundred yards to the boats, but he could barely move. His body had reacted to the loss of heat by shutting down. He was so weak he couldn't shout loud enough to be detected. All he could do was stand there and hope to be found.

The search went on for four hours. Sometime after midnight, the Coast Guard decided it was enough. The captain heard the radio transmission through the speakers, and he listened as the man in charge announced that there were apparently no survivors.

"I knew that for me, it was over, my life as I knew it was about to come to an end," the captain later said.

At about this time, a Kodiak policeman who was sent out to help in the search was walking along the edge of the cliff above the captain. The searcher had a strong handheld flashlight that he was focusing on the rocks below. As the light approached the captain, it caught him directly in the face, and he was rescued.

He was rushed to a hospital in Kodiak, where it was determined that he was suffering from hypothermia. A person is said to be hypothermic when his body temperature falls from the normal 98.6 degrees Fahrenheit to 95 degrees or below. The captain's had dropped to 72 degrees, one of the lowest recorded body temperatures in medical history.

When the captain was interviewed later, he said that even though he had been very cold on the rocks, most of the discomfort left him when hypothermia set in. As his body temperature dropped, he had to bite and pinch himself and *create discomfort* in order to stay awake. His survival depended on staying conscious; if he had drifted off, he would have slipped into the water just as the crewman had.

What's really interesting here is that the captain said he entered a state of euphoria. A warm fuzzy feeling started to overtake him and everything seemed to be OK. "It was like having two or three very stiff drinks," he said.

When I read the captain's story, I realized that – on a mental and emotional level – some type of hypothermia happens to many of us in life. As we engage in our individual lives at work, with our families, in our communities, we enter a mild state of euphoria. If someone asks us how we are doing, we sincerely say, "Just fine."

What I have observed (and experienced for myself) is that, even though we are "doing just fine," we actually have not done anything significantly different for quite awhile. We're in lock step, going through our lives in a numb state of passive indifference. We may seem warm, but we could actually be feeling the deceptive – and potentially deadly – effects of hypothermia.

### *Are we surviving or are we living?*

Many of us deal with change in the same manner as someone exposed to extreme cold: we shut down the system. It's a natural way of coping with change and with life. We don't extend ourselves; we don't grow; we don't take chances; we remain in place.

Only a few months after reading about the captain, I read about a self-help group that sent people out into the wilderness to build confidence through the survival experience. Two of their students had frozen to death during a snowstorm while on a mountain outing.

The tragedy of their deaths was compounded by the fact that there were down-insulated parkas on a log near where they died. If they had put the parkas on, they might have lived. Instead, as hypothermia set in, euphoria took over and they simply froze to death.

Over the years, people have asked me the same two questions: "How do you build confidence?" and "How do you gain security?"

I've noticed that our usual methods for achieving those goals often lead to hypothermic living. Historically, we thought we received our security from wealth, the government, jobs, marriage, or something else outside of ourselves. After four decades of observing human development, I'm convinced that we only become secure by moving toward something.

## It is being in movement toward our goals, our objectives, and our vision that gives us security.

I have talked to countless people who were confident and secure people even though they didn't have the money, the home, the wealth or the prosperity. They were most secure when progressing toward their goals.

The best example I know of this is the story of Reginald. When I first met Reginald, he was a guard, barely making more than the minimum wage. His wife also worked in a low-income job. Reginald worked hard, sometimes putting in 110 hours a week. He and his wife planned it so one of them was home with their children after school or on weekends.

Reginald's goal was to retire with great wealth, which is hard to do on a minimum wage income.

When I first starting talking to Reginald, he and his wife had acquired six rental homes, and the last time we talked, he was up to eleven.

Reginald demonstrates what people can do once they determine a goal and build confidence by moving toward it, instead of choosing to stay in the numbing euphoria of hypothermia.

When we sense hypothermia setting in, it's time to stretch. It is time to set new objectives. It's time to expand our horizons, to push beyond where we are now.

Progress always involves risks. You can't steal second base and keep your foot on first.

**Frederick B. Wilcox**

The best way is to think about growing is not only to observe what we feed ourselves physically – what we eat and drink – but much more importantly, what we feed our *minds*: what we read, what we listen to, the people with whom we associate, and the experiences we create in our minds.

There are many who believe that by the time we are twenty-five it is all over. What we are going to become, what we are, has all been formed and we then live out the remainder of our lives based on what we have learned and experienced to that age. Others, including me, believe that we can continue to grow, continue to experience, continue to become for as long as we wish

A good friend of mine was sitting on the deck of a cruise ship alongside a man who freely admitted that he was in his early eighties. The older man was reading a thick scientific book, and by the title, it appeared to be difficult reading. My friend asked him, "At your age, why are you reading a book like that?" The elderly man said, "Why do you read? Why do you learn?" My friend answered that we learn to earn. The old man replied, *"No, we learn to become."*

As we work our way through hypothermia and whatever form it has taken in our lives, we break through and "learn to become."

### *Incorrect certainties vs. correct uncertainties: why we cling to what we know*

Everyone today must deal with change. I recently attended a seminar in which the presenter, a physician, observed, "A doctor who graduated just ten years ago cannot write 80 percent of the prescriptions necessary to practice effective medicine if, during those ten years, that doctor has not updated his or her skills."

I've heard a chemist put it differently: "A chemist today has 400 percent more 'book learning' than one who graduated just ten years ago."

*To be our most effective, we must constantly renew our skills and knowledge*

A vice president of a large manufacturing firm said: "We are almost better off firing an engineer with ten years experience and hiring a recent college graduate if the engineer with ten years of experience has not continued to learn, to grow and to bring his skills current."

All of these industries, impacted by change, need professionals who renew their skills, not employees who cease to learn. Yet, there is a strong tendency for all of us who have been doing something for a long time to justify our methods. It's almost irresistible to try to prove that the way "we've always done it" is the best way.

**As a matter of course, given the choice to change our minds or prove that we don't have to, we'll usually get busy on the proof.**

Often, we'll stick with the familiar even though such an action defies all logic.

I was in a seminar with a psychiatrist from UCLA who had worked extensively with battered spouses. He was an expert on what he referred to as the "battered spouse syndrome."

When I asked him why a battered spouse would remain with an abusive partner, he said a victim of abuse is often more comfortable with what they know (an *incorrect certainty*), than with taking a chance on something unknown (a *correct uncertainty*).

Even if our present existence is almost unbearable, we tend to fear making choices that will lead us into an unclear future.

**We are much more comfortable with incorrect certainties than we are with the possibility of correct uncertainties.**

The very possibility of a correct uncertainty has a tendency to unnerve us. This is because uncertainty causes us to **Experiment** (stage five in the process of change). Ultimately, our experiment changes us, and that's scary. So we cling to what we know, even if it hurts our income opportunities, diminishes our chances for growth, and limits our relationships.

### Recognize the opportunity in change

How can we make sure to answer when opportunity knocks?

First, don't be so quick to dismiss things. Don't become defensive. Resist the temptation to blame others. When a new opportunity arises, take the time to study it, even if it seems unwelcome at first.

If we don't explore opportunities – even those we think we would rather not engage in – we risk making ourselves obsolete.

In 1960, the July-August *Harvard Business Review* published "Marketing Myopia," by Ted Levitt, an article on change that became a classic. Levitt wrote:

> Every major industry was once a growth industry, but some that are now riding a wave of growth enthusiasm are very much in the shadow of decline. Others, which are thought of as seasoned growth industries, have actually stopped growing. In every case, the reason growth is threatened, slowed, or stopped is not because the market is saturated, it is because there has been a failure of management.
>
> The railroads did not stop growing because the need for passenger and freight transportation declined. The railroads are in trouble today not because others filled the need (cars, truck, airplanes, and even telephones), but because it was not filled by the railroads themselves. They let others take customers away from them because they assumed themselves to be in the railroad business rather than in the transportation business.

Many organizations and individuals have at some point forgotten their purpose. Those who continue to refine and restate their vision will ultimately take advantage of the opportunities change presents.

---

*Sidebar quotes:*

"Too often the opportunity knocks, but by the time we unlatch the chain, push back the bolt, unhook the two locks, and shut off the burglar alarm, it's too late, the opportunity has passed."

**Rita Coolidge**, singer

We get a bigger dream when we let the smaller one die

Change is threatening when it is done *to* us, but it is exciting when it is done *by* us.

We resist change because it means admitting that the way things were done in the past no longer works. It's important to see that the way we did things wasn't wrong; it was right at the time, but circumstances and opportunities change.

**To take advantage of opportunities, we must know when they are presented by changing circumstances; think about what we can do to capitalize on them, and then act.**

## *Summary*

It is being in movement toward our goals, our objectives, and our vision that gives us security.

As a matter of course, given the choice to change our minds or prove that we don't have to, we'll usually get busy on the proof.

We are much more comfortable with incorrect certainties than we are with the possibility of correct uncertainties.

To take advantage of opportunities, we must know when they are presented by changing circumstances, think about what we can do to capitalize on them, and then act.

# Stage Two: Discomfort

As we either gradually "thaw out" or are shocked out of our complacent mindset with a traumatic event, we begin to intuit that something doesn't feel right. This can be a feeling of discomfort or restlessness, and this awareness can occur in any area of our lives: our relationships, our financial situations, our environments, or our careers. Some ignore the signals of discomfort and as the years go by, they become increasingly unhappy. They work hard to block out uneasiness, allotting more and more resources to maintaining the "status quo." At some point, something occurs that pushes us to the next stage.

### *The first step is often the hardest*

When we initiate a process of change and move out of our existing comfort level, we enter an awkward phase. Whenever we learn a new skill, there will be a dreadful, frustrating stage.

Some people are so afraid of having other people see them fumble that they resist even taking a chance that would make them enter this stage.

Effective individuals – those who want to develop their confidence, their skills, and achieve a high level of functionality – realize that the discomfort is part of the price of success. They are willing to look awkward, and maybe even silly, in order to move to new levels of accomplishment.

**Effective individuals are willing to appear inept at first, realizing that if they stay with it, they will become proficient.**

33

There is something about human nature that I refer to (with apologies to George Lucas) as "the force." The force stops us before we get started. It puts up tremendous resistance. Often we give up right before we get to the easy part.

Think about it: When we resolve to do something, the first step is the usually hardest.

It gets easier once you get past the first step

In long distance running, for example, the first and second miles are always the most difficult. Yet, people go out day after day, do the hardest part, and then quit.

The same applies to quitting smoking and losing weight. Those first five or ten days are the hardest. How many people struggle through those, give up, and then go back to smoking and eating? We keep doing the hard part over and over!

Another thing we tend to do when we start something new is look around to see how other people are doing. Instead of concentrating on our own efforts, we see people we perceive are doing "better" than us and get discouraged. We are so scared of appearing awkward in comparison that we stop focusing on the objective: our own personal growth.

We will never become what we could become if we insist on always playing it safe. If we are going to continue to grow, we must push past our previous levels of accomplishment and move out of our so-called comfort zones.

### What are you conditioned to do?

When we feel uncomfortable about change, it's important to understand that much of what we do is a result of conditioning.

Do you remember basic psychology, when they explained Pavlov and his famous experiment with the dog? Pavlov rings the bell, turns on the light, feeds the

34

dog some meat, and conditions the dog to associate the bell and the light with the meat. Eventually, to get the dog to salivate, all that's necessary is to ring a bell or turn on a light!

Sometimes we become so conditioned to a certain way of doing things, we don't even *think* about changing.

In the 1970s Werner Erhard was a very powerful student and teacher of change. In his well-known est seminars, Erhard strove to point out how powerfully conditioning affects our ability to understand and successfully manage change.

In his presentations, Erhard developed a signature story about mice and cheese that perfectly illustrated this difference. Years later, Dr. Spencer Johnson wrote the bestselling book *Who Moved My Cheese?* based on Erhard's story.

As Werner Erhard told it, a group of scientists conducted an experiment with a mouse. They didn't feed the little thing for twenty-four hours and then put it in an opening in front of five tunnels.

They placed some cheese down tunnel number three. The mouse could smell it, but didn't know which tunnel contained it. He went down tunnel one, then tunnel five, and then finally down tunnel three. The mouse got his fill of the cheese, came back out and was put away for another twenty-four hours.

The next morning they put the cheese in tunnel three and the mouse again went down several wrong tunnels before finding it. After seven or eight days, the mouse learned, and went straight down tunnel number three.

After a couple of months, they moved the cheese to a different tunnel. The next morning, the mouse went down tunnel number three. He became frustrated upon finding no cheese, eventually came out, and went down a few tunnels before finding the cheese in tunnel number one.

The scientists continued to place the cheese in tunnel number one. It only took the mouse a few days to realize that they had moved the cheese. It stopped going down tunnel number three and began to go down tunnel number one.

But as Erhard explained, the difference between the mouse and most of us is that even though the cheese has been moved from tunnel three to tunnel number one, we will *persist* in going down tunnel number three.

If we don't find the cheese, we become agitated, frustrated and anxious. We feel that if we complain loudly enough, they will move the cheese back to tunnel number three. The truth is, we can gripe all we want; they aren't moving the cheese back.

After a meeting at which I shared Erhard's story, a woman came up to me. She said she wished her daughter could have been there to hear my presentation.

She explained that she and her husband had a lovely and bright daughter. Unfortunately, as the daughter grew up, they had spoiled her. Whenever she wanted something, she would pout and sulk and invariably get her way.

The woman said that their daughter had met a wonderful young man in college who she later married. Whenever she wanted her way, the newlywed wife would pout and sulk as conditioned.

During the time that she was engaged to the young man, it had been endearing to him. After a year of marriage, however, there was a change.

Her mother told me: "Last weekend, they were over for dinner, and our daughter started to pout and sulk. I looked over at her husband, and almost imperceptibly, darkness appeared in his eyes. What used to be cute and fun, what had added a sparkle to their love, has become a source of irritation to him. If our daughter chooses not to change, their marriage will be in jeopardy."

"You see, he has moved the cheese."

Cheese moving happens all the time, in interpersonal relationships, marriages, and especially in business today. In the discomfort stage, it may either be time for us to "move our own cheese," or to realize that someone else around us already has.

### Don't regret the past – it's what brought you here

In the first half of my life, I experienced tumultuous change. I may not be alone in being able to say I have been a thief and a millionaire, a CEO and an alcoholic. But I suspect I may be in a marginally smaller group when I say the lessons I learned in my early years led to a much more effective way of dealing with change in the second part of my life.

In order to make sense of and pass on the lessons of that part of my life, I once wrote a letter to our grown son, Jon. It began:

"Well, Jon…

…now that you are a husband, father, homemaker and sales manager, you have come a long way. Now that you are in your forties, you are experiencing with your sons many of the things I experienced with you.

If anyone were to rate sons and fathers on a scale of one to ten, you would receive a high ten as a son and you'd be off the chart as a father.

I'd like to share with you some experiences from my life that have been great learning experiences.

I was twenty-eight when you were born. Fortunately, by that time in my life, I had achieved a great deal of stability and, some would say, success.

As you were growing up, you saw me in a number of impressive roles. I was an executive vice president of a growing corporation and later a corporate president. You saw me traveling and presiding over what we then thought were very important meetings with political leaders, civic groups and business executives. You saw me fly to Washington, D.C. to address Congressional committees, and you saw me attending great receptions, dinners and conferences where I was often asked to speak.

You know that I became a marathon runner in my forties and I am still running them in my seventies, and how you and the rest of the family thought I was a little daft when I went to parachute out of an airplane at age fifty. It wasn't really skydiving, just jumping out of an airplane with a parachute hooked to the static line, but it was a feat for a person with claustrophobia and fear of heights.

I remember the many summers you and I spent fishing on the ocean, running our charter boat, two of the finest salmon fishermen to ever cast a line. I had to be the captain, because I had the U.S. Coast Guard license, but you were a great first mate, and treated the charters as if they were the most important people in the world.

But Jon, it wasn't always like that. I have made a lot of choices, and a lot of them were bad. There is a dark side to my past. Though few people know about them, those darker experiences are thread in the fabric of who I am.

I don't want to dwell in the past but neither do I wish to shut the door on it, because the past is what brought me here today and made me, among other things, a lucky father.

All day, every day, we have the opportunity to make good decisions. As I look back, I see that the friends I chose rate very high on the list of what has influenced my life.

When I was fourteen, I chose to hang out with boys a couple of years older than me. They were seasoned young men, and they liked to smoke and drink.

The bad choices started when we set out to burglarize a tavern. Though I was only fifteen at the time, the pattern had started and my course for many years was set. We barely escaped getting caught. Our loot wasn't cigarettes or money, but wine.

We kept stealing, and every time I escaped getting caught, it made it easier the next time. At that point, I had become a criminal and was on my way to becoming an alcoholic.

But it sure was fun to hang out with those guys.

One time we made a large snowball, about two feet in diameter and packed very tightly, and dropped it off an overpass onto a moving car. I don't know how much damage was done, but I know it was the stupidest thing, the cruelest thing we had ever done up until then, the one with the most potential for tragedy.

It was a matter of time before several of my friends were caught. For some, there was no leniency. They were not sent to a juvenile home, but ended up in the county jail or prison.

I didn't intend to be a "fence," but when an acquaintance (not one of our regular threesome) named Jack and his two friends broke into a liquor warehouse and stole cases of Budweiser, I fenced them. Of course, they got caught. The police didn't contact me about this. I'm not sure this should be considered lucky because when you don't get caught, you just keep on making those bad decisions.

By that time, alcohol had me in its grip. At nineteen, when I entered the Navy, I was a full-blown alcoholic.

I was completely self-absorbed. Life as I knew it evolved from and revolved around my need for alcohol. Even after I stopped drinking at age twenty-four, I had long periods of total self-centeredness. I was totally immersed in my own drama.

I now realize that I was following the path of my father, my uncle, and possibly one of my older brothers. Fortunately, the genetically inherited disease of alcoholism seems to have passed you, but know that this carries in our family. My father, your grandfather, although he was a wonderful man, was totally caught up in his own alcoholism.

He died on skid row in a "flop house," in a tiny room with a bathroom down the hall. I remember it clearly; I was eighteen, had just graduated from high school and was working at the time. A neighborhood couple and I were the only people at his funeral. Your grandfather died young, in his mid-fifties. I'm sure that if I had continued to drink and smoke, I would have lived no longer than he did.

Your Uncle Art, my older brother, also had a great influence on me. I remember the Friday after Thanksgiving, 1947. Art was seventeen and I was fifteen. Our mother had left the house to go to work and I was about to leave to sell papers at my stand downtown. The last thing I remember before leaving the house that day was seeing my brother lying across our mother's bed. He said he was having trouble with his legs. He was very macho, and being older, had very little to do with me. He was frightened because his legs had started to go numb.

The following Monday, Art entered the hospital and was diagnosed with Multiple Sclerosis. He became totally immobilized and almost died. Fortunately, the disease went into remission and he was able to walk with a cane after a couple of years.

In the hospital, I told Art that I was thinking of quitting high school and going to work full time. He played the only card he had. I still recall his words, over fifty years later: "I have never asked you for anything in my life, but I'm going to ask you to stay in high school and finish it and become the first person in our family to graduate."

The only reason that I finished high school was because of what my brother said to me.

After I graduated, the Korean War was just starting and I had a choice to get drafted into the Army or enlist in the Navy. I chose the Navy and that's the time of my life when my alcoholism took over.

I became a pathological drinker. I drove drunk, which I think is one of the worst things a person can do. I knew that alcohol would do the same thing to me that it did to your grandfather, but I just didn't care; I was having too much fun.

It's a wonder I survived. I'm lucky that the Navy punished me as little as it did. I was discharged when I was twenty-three, and I came home and married your mother.

Alcoholism still had a stranglehold on me. I lasted through three weeks of the spring quarter at the University of Washington in my freshman year under the GI bill before the police got me for drunk driving. I went back to see the judge again and again and again. The fact that I never injured or killed anyone is enough to make me spend every day of my life being grateful.

I dropped out of college and went to work at a marketing agency owned by Moses ("Moe") Dinner.

The downhill spiral continued to accelerate. I was often late for work, nursing a hangover. I was finally sentenced to a long period in jail. I served my time in the police farm for alcoholics. I was twenty-four.

My boss Moe Dinner fired me, of course. But he also helped me. He had heard Eric Bergman, purchasing manager of Rainier Brewing Company (later President of the National Purchasing Management Association) speak about his alcoholism. Moe was so impressed with Eric's story of his recovery, he insisted I make contact with Eric. I did, and this led to my successfully dealing with my alcoholism. Seventeen years later, I was a millionaire and executive vice-president of a very successful company.

The story could stop there, but I had a need to put my prosperity in the ditch, and that's just what I did.

When our corporation and the CEO went bankrupt, I decided against filing for bankruptcy myself. Because I decided not to go into bankruptcy, everyone came after me. I remember the night I came home and saw that the sheriff had nailed the eviction notice on our door.

We lost our beautiful home and ended up in that rented two-bedroom house. I think it would have been all right except for the time when your sisters were trying to sleep in the basement and that rat scurried overhead on the rafters when the lights were still on. Living in that rented home was a big adventure after what we had become accustomed to. But let's face it, Jon, a lot of people live in a rented two-bedroom home and feel very fortunate to have it. That's the way I felt.

They say when people get into difficult situations, such as losing their financial wherewithal, it's important that they have the support of those who love them. You and your two sisters, Sherry and Cynthia, were absolutely amazing during this time. Sherry continued with school, worked part-time after school, and then learned baking as a profession. Cynthia, who worked as a bag girl at Safeway, was, like you and Sherry, an incredible source of strength for me.

Since you were so young at the time, I don't know if you know how I started over again. I worked out of the front seat of my car and used a payphone at a Union Oil gas station. That car was my office, but even so, I acted prosperous. Meanwhile, I was being sued with a high degree of regularity. It seemed like I was getting served two or three times a week.

As you know, I made it back to prosperity. We have a beautiful home again and I've paid off all the people I owed.

It's been thirty-seven years since then, and although I know there's always a possibility I might put it in the ditch again, I'm making choices that put the odds in my favor.

I lived with the fear of losing everything, Jon. I didn't think you deserved to be bogged down with my challenges and heartaches, so I didn't confide in you. Now that you are an adult, you must face your own challenges in life. It may help you to know a little of what I was thinking and learning.

"Never tell your troubles to anyone. Eighty-five percent don't care and the other fifteen percent are glad."

**Old saying**

Going through it wasn't any worse than the fears that you have when you're not grounded in business or in life. The fear of uncertainty, of losing your health, your prosperity, or your happiness; the fear of not having the house, the big car, the titles – I saw that it's all so meaningless, so empty, so senseless.

In fact, the truly great lessons were those I learned after I went sideways. I learned not to regret the past or shut the door on it. I learned that when life hands you a challenge, it is the ego that suffers and causes most of the pain. I learned that failure offers a wonderful opportunity to study what happened, learn from it, and re-invent yourself.

I learned that I should save 10 percent off the top, give away all I can, be nicer to people, continue to read and study, and if I get knocked silly, that's fine. I learned that all the bad stuff I went through made it possible for me to make new choices. I chose to find new friends, to read good books, and listen to people who were successful.

When I think back on it, in addition to losing our wealth, the experience of hitting bottom a second time in my life also caused me to lose a lot of things that were holding me back. I lost my fear of economic uncertainty. I lost my fear of people. After we lost everything financially, I no longer had to lie awake wondering what it would be like to lose everything we had. I don't particularly recommend the route I took, but having been through it, I know I never have to be afraid of that again.

*When the worst happened, I lost my fear of it*

To live in fear of the banker, the competition, the trends in the marketplace, proved to be nothing more than a useless expenditure of my limited energy. In fact, my worries were a way of holding off the changes I was naturally growing toward.

There is a marvelous line in Proverbs that warns about wealth that is gained too quickly, and the lesson for me of course is that whether it is quick or takes a long period of time, it's critically important that you make it right in your own mind to become prosperous. While a lot of people might not say that seventeen years is too quick, it sure seemed to happen that way. This time, the wealth, the prosperity, the success, confidence, and the happiness have come ever so slowly.

*To stay prosperous, I must make it right in my own mind to be prosperous*

I don't know if I'm going to be financially wiped out again, but I do know that I'm not going to spend one minute worrying about it.

My life so far has been a great adventure and I wanted to put it down and share it with you and the rest of the family.

They say you are just about as safe as your secrets, Jon. After this, I don't have many secrets left. In fact, I think I'm down to just about zero, which has, in itself, an incredible amount of freedom.

*One of the most precious things we are granted is the power of choice*

I created my universe. Yes, there is always the element of chance, but chance has played such a very small part in my experience. Most of it, I created by goals that I set and choices that I made.

**When I realized that I could rewrite the script and create anything I wanted, if I wanted to pay the price, it added a new dimension to my freedom.**

We are free to choose how to lead our life, what to think, with whom we want to spend our time, what we want to read and experience.

If I don't like my life as I am experiencing it today, I can create just about any life I want... and so can you.

Love, Dad

### *You wrote your script, you can rewrite it*

I wrote that letter as a result of a wonderful gift I was given one day at our monthly Executive Roundtable. The ten business owners and managers of our group meet to discuss and analyze problems in our companies. Every other month, we read a book related to business or a biography and discuss it.

At one meeting, Ty Traub, a member of the roundtable who owns a drywall installation company, quoted something he had read recently:

**"You never have to wonder what you want to be when you grow up; just look around, you are already it."**

Many of us, even after we have "grown up," really want to do something else. We'd rather be a fireman, a cowgirl, an author, an entrepreneur. One thing is certain: When we look around and assess our current situation, we often conclude, *"Whatever it is I am going to become, this probably isn't it!"*

Guess what? We are what we have made ourselves. We have written our own scripts, so it is a perfect realization to see what we already are. This is what we have built, this is what we have decided upon in our own minds already. Of course, there are people and circumstances that have altered our lives, and there is always the element of chance, but nonetheless, where we are in our lives is no accident.

Continuing with his presentation, Ty said: "Our life is not some cruel hoax; it's a matter of choice that we are doing what we are doing; it's the result of what has gone on before and decisions we've made that have led us to this point in our life.

**"The great news is that if we don't like the script we have written, we can rewrite it anytime we are so inclined."**

As living, thinking beings, we have a tremendous power to choose. The power of choice is the strongest and the most important control we have. We can decide to create something that is meaningful to us as individuals. Almost everything we are experiencing today – the life we are leading – is based on the choices we've made in the past. That being true, *we can create any future we want based on the decisions we make today.*

Beginning that day, I chose to reinvent my life by understanding how I got to where I was, how I had written and re-written my own script, and how I had the power to write it for the future.

## Today starts a new chapter

In the second stage of change, **Discomfort**, we recognize that something isn't right. It's common to take the first wavelets of awareness and immediately use them to feel bad about our choices and our lives. You say to yourself, "I should have done this, I should have done that!"

I want to suggest that the mistakes, failures, disappointments, and frustrations of the past don't make a difference now. It doesn't matter how disgracefully we have behaved. It doesn't matter how mediocre or how successful our life has been. We don't need to slam the door on the past, but we need to stop the endless preoccupation with what "should have been." The past is what brought us to today, and today starts a new chapter.

*The past brought us to today, and today begins a new chapter*

We can take control, take out a clean sheet of paper, and write a new script for ourselves.

## Summary

Effective individuals are willing to appear inept at first, realizing that if they stay with it, they will become proficient.

I don't want to dwell on the past but neither do I wish to shut the door on it, because the past is what brought me here today.

You never have to wonder what you want to be when you grow up, just look around; you are already it.


The great news is that if we don't like the script we have written, we can rewrite it anytime we are so inclined.

# Stage Three: Analysis

In this stage, we begin careful examination of the situation. The idea that a change might be happening is considered. This stage is filled with questions. "What's going on?" "Why do things feel different?" "What's making me uncomfortable?"

There is also a great deal of resistance in this stage, usually motivated by the need to feel that we are right and others are to blame.

### "Ralphie's law" and our need to be right

While working with a group of managers, I posed the question, "What is the dominant, single greatest motivating force known to humankind?" One participant said, "Well, of course, it was Sigmund Freud who said, 'The strongest motivating force is *sex*.'" A few nodded their heads.

Someone else then volunteered that the reason Freud split with Alfred Adler was that Adler felt it was not sex, but the quest for *power*

Others suggested that Viktor Frankl got the blue ribbon when he said that humanity's greatest desire is to search for *meaning and purpose.*

While sex, power and meaning are great motivators, I've noticed that the *great need to be right about what we believe* is also near the top of the list.

I've often wondered why it's so difficult to change. Many of us feel that "If I am willing to change, it means that I am wrong. It means I've made a mistake, that I've been living a lie." This attitude creates a tremendous motivation for us to be right.

Our *need to be right* is so powerful that

- We would rather be right than be successful
- We would rather be right than be happy
- We would rather be right than have good relations with our children
- We would rather be right than have a positive relationship with our boss, with our team members, or our spouse

We resist change that would benefit us because we feel it is an admission that we were wrong in the past

In my career as a management trainer, I've worked with many salespeople who felt that it is much more important to be right than to make sales! They form an opinion about something such as the competency of their boss and they go down the rabbit hole. It's more important to prove that their boss is inept than it is for them to be prosperous and successful!

Looking back on forty-seven years of marriage, I understand that the root of any disagreement or disharmony on my part was about "who is right." After learning this, I have often asked myself the question, "Do I want to have a warm, harmonious, peaceful home and a happy marriage, or do I want to be right?" In some cases, it is impossible to do both.

As I studied and thought about Freud, Adler and Frankl, I jokingly started referring to my point of view as "Ralphie's Law":

## One of the strongest motivating forces known to humankind is the need to be right.

As we move into the **Analysis** stage, it's important to understand this law. As we examine our life situations, there is a powerful urge to resist change that would benefit us because it would be an admission that we were wrong in the past.

Changing, even for the better, carries an *emotional price* that for some is hard to pay. We have a built-in resistance.

To carry through with change, we must convince ourselves that doing things differently does not mean that we should feel stupid or inadequate for our past or current choices.

**It is helpful to realize that the choices we made were good at the time we made them with the information we had; but the information and times have changed.**

Some time ago, I encountered a young man who told me a great story that perfectly illustrates Ralphie's Law. I had finished my morning workout at my athletic club and was standing at the washbasin, shaving. A young man stood next to me, also shaving.

I introduced myself and we chatted. He told me he was an accountant who worked for a large firm. He said his job required him to travel and that whenever possible, his wife accompanied him.

I told him I found this interesting, since I rarely met men whose wives travel with them. He started to explain that his wife owned a boutique. She liked to get ideas from art galleries. Then he confessed the real reason she traveled with him was because of something that had happened six months into their marriage, when he was sent to another city for a three-day project.

Being newlyweds, he and his wife didn't look forward to their first separation. They took solace in the thought that he was only scheduled to be away for three days. But it turned out the project took a little longer than anticipated. One extension of a couple of days followed after another, and weeks went by.

During this stretch, he thought of flying home on a weekend to see his wife, but his clients needed him to work Saturdays and Sundays. He thought about flying his wife down to see him, but it always seemed like the project was on the verge of completion in a few more days. Also, the firm was unwilling to pay for her airfare and he thought he probably shouldn't spend his money because he would be home soon. He finally returned home on a Saturday afternoon after being away for six weeks.

That evening, he sat down to the dinner that his beautiful wife had prepared. She had the finest steak she could find along with his favorite salad, candles and wine. She sat across the table from him, all dressed up, and it seemed as if they were back on their honeymoon.

Looking at me in the mirror with a rueful smile, he told me that his wife made a comment about something financial, and he said, "No, that's not the way it is," disagreeing with her gently. She affirmed her position. So then he said, "But I know I'm right because I'm a CPA." Her response was, "I know I'm right because I read it in the newspaper."

The dinner deteriorated, as did the rest of the evening. "That night and the next two nights, I slept on the sofa," the accountant told me.

"And that's why she travels with me now," he said. "There was so much tension built up between us because of that separation that whenever possible, we now try to never be apart."

His own point was about marriage and separation, but what he was really teaching me about was our burning need to be right. It can be more important than a welcome home celebration and a perfectly cooked meal with your wife. It can be so important that you end up sleeping on the sofa.

Let's face it: Being right is one of the most satisfying things in the world. Another way to look at it is to say that being wrong is one of the most unsettling.

That's why it's a real blow to the ego to feel that we have made a mistake. That's why people sometimes don't want to change. It would mean admitting they are wrong. Many of us believe that if we just keep on long enough with our misconceived behavior, we will make it right. Despite all other indicators, we believe that reality will give in to our viewpoint rather than vice versa.

My experience is that, sooner or later, reality wins.

## This great need to be right is what stops many of us from changing.

Think about these questions:

- Do I want to be right or do I want to have a happy marriage?
- Do I want to be right or do I want to be successful?
- Do I want to be right or do I want to be prosperous?

Shortly after my discussion with the young CPA, my wife and I were living on a cliff high above the water with a marvelous view. By this time, our children were grown and gone. It was a lovely spring evening. A soft breeze drifted in from the water as the sun slowly sank behind the mountains to the west. As we were standing out in the backyard admiring the view, my wife and I could hear waves breaking softly on the beach below.

My wife turned to me and said, "The tide is making a lot of noise as it is coming in this evening."

I said, "That's not the tide. It's the wake caused by a ship that we didn't see; it passed perhaps ten minutes ago and the wake has finally reached the beach."

She said, "No, that's not the wake, that's the tide coming in. You are gone a great deal and I'm here alone and I hear it often. That is the tide coming in."

At this point, I reminded her that I used to be a licensed charter boat captain. I had to pass a very difficult examination, and I learned all about the tides and the water. I said, "As a matter of fact, the tide is silent, you never hear it coming in. What you hear is the wave action that is caused by the wind or the wake of a ship."

She said, "No, I am positive that it is the tide."

I opened my mouth to tell her I was right and she was wrong. Then I remembered my friend, the CPA, and what happened on his homecoming dinner when he insisted he was right. With great tenderness in my voice, I said, "Darling, what we hear this evening may be the loudest tide ever recorded in marine history."

She turned her eyes to me and said, "I may have married truly the smartest man ever, a true genius."

My new CPA acquaintance was a great teacher.

I had no need to sleep on the sofa that night.

## *Once you start to blame, there is no end to it*

When the marketplace changes, the customer changes, a relationship changes, or people around us change, it can be disconcerting. We often feel the temptation to blame others for our misfortune.

But blaming others, although it might offer temporary satisfaction, gets us nowhere. Until we begin to look at our own actions, we will remain stuck in place. Faulting others is an especially dangerous maneuver because it easily becomes a way of life. As we work our way through the **Analysis** stage, it is important to avoid the blaming trap.

*Blaming others for whatever happens to us can easily become a conditioned response*

I can think of no one better to illustrate the perils of laying blame on others than a salesman named Richard.

I met Richard when one of my clients referred him to me. Richard had been with the company a long time and was the number two salesman. Richard's bosses told me that he had always rubbed people the wrong way and lately had become moody and difficult. In meetings, he stared blankly at the wall, was unresponsive, and sometimes even walked out.

One of the managers I spoke to considered Richard a friend and said that outside of work he was a nice, warm guy, but at work he had become a "nightmare" to be around. He also told me that Richard had created some financial pressures for himself, having moved into a big house in an upscale neighborhood. Perhaps most significantly, he told me that their business had changed from a consultative to a transactional business, but that Richard had not changed with it.

"When you blame others, you give up your power to change."

**Anonymous**

In my practice, I often encounter people who tell me, "The company has changed." Richard knew the chorus to that song very well. In our sessions he often told me that the firm had once been like a family, but now it was just plain big.

My first meeting with Richard was a marvelous and exciting experience. He told me that he thought of the company as a team and of himself as a team member. At the same time, he said that he was living with a tremendous fear that his success was going to unravel, that the work he had was going to disappear.

At one time, Richard had made over $250,000 a year. When he saw me, his income had been reduced to half of that. When I asked Richard how he had made $250,000 a year, he said that his success had been a result of hard work and being in the right place at the right time. When I asked him why he felt his income had declined, he had a ready answer: Everything had changed – his company, his customers, and the market.

"46% of those who quit their jobs last year did so because they felt unappreciated."

*U.S. Dept. of Labor, 1996*

His failure, as he explained it, was due to outside reasons and had nothing to do with the fact that he wasn't working hard anymore. His bosses had told me that Richard was given the state of California as part of his sales territory. After a year, he hadn't visited or even made any calls to the state, even though it could have been a lucrative territory. I was told that Richard spent a lot of time reading in the office. The executive vice president said that it seemed Richard had become immobilized.

When I asked Richard why he was so unhappy at his job, he said it was his boss, the regional manager. At one point, the manager had harshly told Richard, "You're washed up in this business." Richard had let his manager's words fester inside.

One of Richard's core issues was that he couldn't trust anyone because his father was an alcoholic and had let him down. Whenever I hear a story like this, I wonder: Is that a reason to fail or is that a reason to succeed?

Many of the millions of us who have had an alcoholic caregiver are still getting mileage out of it decades later. It is difficult to grow up with a parent in that condition. At the same time, I believe we have choices. One is to seek help and work our way through the pain and frustration we may feel. We may come to view our backgrounds as reasons to be extra motivated. Another choice is to milk our backgrounds and use them as a reason for mediocrity or failure.

Richard felt a lot of unresolved anger at the regional management and the office in California. He felt betrayed by the regional manager. He said he couldn't talk to his manager about his problems because the manager was authoritative and wouldn't listen. It had reached the point where after one blow-up, the regional manager called the corporate office and said: "I can't take this anymore. Richard has to leave or I will."

Underlying Richard's anger was fear – fear for his family, fear of losing his house, fear of losing his lifestyle. He had funded his children's educations, but with high mortgage payments and a standard of living more than he could afford, he was living in dread.

I've seen people who have tremendous insecurity and fear find a way to harness their fear and become very successful. They use fear as a tool to propel them to outstanding performance.

I've noticed that people who seem to be prosperous, myself included, lack confidence but have something that drives them. For a long time, I denied that I lacked confidence. I projected that I was a supremely confident individual in leadership positions, seminars and business relationships. I was actually compensating for my perceived shortcomings and inner demons. To dispel these doubts and apprehensions, I focused on my strengths – I relived my positive, successful experiences. I wrote about them, documented them and studied them. And then I went back to doing the things that made the successful experiences possible.

Our inner demons and self-doubts can be used to our advantage

Others become immobilized by their fear. They lash out, withdraw, or in Richard's case, develop an anger that impairs performance.

Life is about choices. I can choose to become angry and blame anyone I want: my parents, boss, spouse, the president of the company, or the president of the United States. The list is endless.

Or I can choose to generate incredible positive energy and use it to help me become healthy, prosperous and happy.

For those of us who want to use change and harness it, it is imperative that we return to the basics that made us successful in the first place. In Richard's case, he had stopped doing the things that had once made him such a high achiever.

When I reviewed Richard's skills and aptitudes, it was clear to me that he still had the capability for great success. He had strong verbal skills, a superior intellect and an exceptional appearance. He held two university degrees and had completed some post-graduate work. He'd held a range of positions, which afforded him vast experience. And yet, blaming others had halved his income and made his life miserable.

I suggested that he start writing a journal, focusing on all the positive things he had going for him, especially the successful experiences.

I suggested to Richard that he embrace two objectives. One would be to find peace with himself and those around him, and the second to become very prosperous. If Richard repeated what he had done before, he could double his income. And he could have peace if he so chose.

Richard decided to change. He made a complete inventory of his successful experiences, which then became assets on his balance sheet.

He went to his regional manager, apologized, and said that he would change. He kept a careful diary of how he was spending his time. He established clear-cut goals, wrote them out, made visuals, taped them to his wall, and recorded this progress in his journal. He thought about what had made him successful in the past and went back to doing it.

Most importantly, he started treating his colleagues with respect and strived to be gracious in every interpersonal contact.

The result of all this work? Richard began to earn even more than he had previously. Just as importantly, he changed the habits that had caused him and those around him misery.

### Anger is a poor choice over peace

Another block to change, similar to blaming others, is *anger*. I have asked myself many times:

"Anger is a short madness."

**Horace ,**
*Latin poet*

- Is anger ever justified?
- What are the costs of anger?
- How much harm does getting angry do to the person experiencing the emotion?
- Does expressing anger ever help to motivate other people?
- Is anger a valuable behavior?

With a few exceptions, it's a personal choice to display anger. Yes, some people are born with "different wiring" and are predisposed to anger and depression because of biological reasons or emotional dysfunction. For most of us though, anger is a choice. We choose when and where to become angry.

"Anger is a weed, hate is the tree."

**St. Augustine of Hippo,**
*Christian theologian*

People sometimes elect to deal with difficult circumstances in their lives by displaying some form of retaliation or negativity. They get annoyed, write letters, complain to their boss or anyone who will listen, and most likely will avoid the person with whom they are irritated. They will do anything to let their ire be known.

Becoming angry and spouting it out verbally is not a solution for me. Becoming irritated, snappish, and explosive is counterproductive. It's the worst possible thing for me because expressing anger often fuels more rage. What helps me is to step back and interpret the incident that has upset me for what it is – simply one event in my life.

*If we can't control it, we can control our reactions to it*

We have a finite amount of time and energy. I have learned it is best to use that time to find peace. Instead of getting angry over things that have happened to us, let's use that energy to develop the resources to become emotionally and financially prosperous.

## Many of our greatest teachers come disguised as difficult, rude, or mean-spirited people

When someone treats us in a manner that raises our ire, it might be better to take a breath and think about what we can learn from the experience.

Everyone is a teacher, and some valuable lessons come when you least expect them. Some of the best teachers are those who show us what *not* to do.

Of course, when we are face to face with a difficult person, we don't welcome them as a valuable teacher – we simply find them unpleasant. We often need time and perspective to discover the lessons they offer. A little empathy and kindness can speed up the learning process.

**Consider difficult people the greatest gift you have received that day, because they are teaching you something valuable.**

While running on a beautiful mid-winter Sunday morning, I discovered I had something to teach someone else.

As I ran along the waterfront, the morning sunlight sparkled on the calm waters of Puget Sound and I could clearly view the snow-covered mountains that surround Seattle. A thousand-foot freighter lumbered through the water, dwarfing the numerous sail and powerboats out enjoying the day.

On the road, a seemingly endless string of trucks rattled by, heading to where I guessed a large freighter was loading. It was amazing how many trucks were out on that Sunday morning, given that there was so little other traffic. I estimated there were hundreds of trucks at work moving the containers from the staging area to the pier to be loaded onto the vessel.

I noticed that many of the truck drivers were not attentive to their driving. They were drinking coffee, doing paperwork, talking on their radios or phones. More than a few looked like they'd had a rough Saturday night.

There was no sidewalk but I stayed well off the road on the shoulder. The traffic heading in the opposite direction from me was driving into the sun. From experience, I knew that it was very difficult to see ahead on this road when the sun in is that particular position. Thinking about that fact, I moved a little farther onto the shoulder.

Up ahead, I saw a runner coming toward me, which was unusual because it is not a popular route for runners. He ran with his back to the trucks that drove into the bright morning sun. As I approached him, I saw that he was running on the white line, just on the edge of the southbound lane.

When I was a couple of blocks away from him, I realized that I knew something that he didn't – the people driving past him from behind were blinded by the sun.

When I got about twenty-five yards from him, I noticed that he had on a Walkman and seemed to be unaware of the traffic, or much of anything else. As we approached each other, I acknowledged him by waving and saying, "Good morning." He fumbled on his belt for the switch on his Walkman. I slowed down a little and when we were almost abreast of each other, I asked him: "Would it be all right to tell you something?"

He gave me a dirty look and continued running. When he got about five or ten yards past me, he looked back and yelled, *"What?"* It was more of a snarl than a question. He kept running and soon was out of earshot.

I wanted to tell him that he was putting himself in danger. I wanted to share with him that the last thing many of the truck drivers and tourists on the road that day expected to encounter was a runner six inches off their right front fender.

I thought about it over the last couple of miles of my run that morning. The runner seemed angry that I had spoken to him. I don't know why, but that's not important. His anger kept him from receiving information that would have increased his personal safety.

I felt some anger at his rudeness and stupidity too, until I realized there was a lesson for me in this encounter. It occurred to me that perhaps I had been snappish at times in my life when others had something important to teach me.

I realized that when someone appears to be non-threatening and approaches me with something to share, maybe I should take the time to pause and listen. When someone makes the effort to tell me something, perhaps they see something from their side of the road that I don't.

### Wherever I go, I take me with me

Sometimes, during the **Analysis** stage, it becomes clear that we have a choice of staying in a "burned out" situation or moving on.

There is a temptation to drop everything and light out for the territories. While I understand this desire, I don't think it usually leads to the best outcome. Whatever problems you pack up in one place will only be unpacked when you get wherever you are going.

> If I keep doing what I've been doing, I'm bound to keep getting what I've been getting

If you don't come to peace with your current situation, you will often end up repeating the same mistakes down the road.

## We are bound to keep following our own mess until we get it right.

I have become convinced that it is more rewarding – though not necessarily easier – to become successful in our existing job and relationship rather than to move on.

I counsel people that after you have become successful "here" and you still want to move on, do it with the freedom and the knowledge that you are going on to a new adventure from a success rather than a failure.

### Give yourself permission to succeed

In the last part of the **Analysis** stage, when we stop blaming others and do away with our need to be right, when we understand that embracing change today does not necessarily mean we disqualify our lives up to this point, we are in a position to begin to answer our own questions. "What's going on?" "Why don't I make as much money?" "Why does my husband seem less engaged?" 'Why don't I enjoy my work anymore?"

We can start by looking at our failures, where there is much to learn. Like examining the facets of a diamond, we can turn our failure around and look at it from every possible angle. After we have gleaned from it what we can, we place the experience in a mental file drawer and lock it away. Then we substitute a mental re-creation of "what went right" during our *successful* experience.

While we should study our failures to learn, it is important to resist the temptation to dwell on them, or on future failures. Don't immerse yourself in what you don't want to happen.

## When we worry, we are visualizing that which we hope will not occur.

As has been written many times, worry is setting in vibrant color and 3D form the very thing we don't want to happen. It's to our advantage to substitute the alternative: the positive, successful outcomes we've had and can readily envision.

If we understand our successes, we increase the odds of being able to repeat them

While failure is a great teacher, we can learn infinitely more from our successes. Remember Richard, the salesman who came out of a tailspin and more than doubled his income? He documented his successes in a journal. If we study, relive, re-create, and re-taste our accomplishments, we come to understand them. If we come to understand how we achieved them, we make it much more probable that we will enjoy new successes.

At this stage, it becomes tempting to stave off change by telling ourselves we aren't ready; we need to gain more knowledge. The truth is, we already have all of the wisdom and intelligence that we will ever need to succeed.

Many of us wait for other people to give us *permission* to succeed. We want their approval. But we don't need to wait for anyone else to give us the green light; any time we want, we can give ourselves permission to make a positive change.

## Tap into what you already know

The tools of success are often not money, social standing or superior knowledge. Success can come from the natural process of allowing ourselves to learn from our experiences.

For example, I find great books to be a wonderful source of knowledge and inspiration. But I have often observed I am not actually learning anything new. When I read, what is really happening is a *rediscovery* of the experience and wisdom that I already have.

Sometimes seeking knowledge or training, especially from the wrong teacher, can be a hindrance to the natural process of learning from our experiences.

When our son Jon started playing baseball, he couldn't get a hit. I practiced with him for hours. When I took him to his little league games, I agonized over how he would do. When he went up to bat, he would stand in the batter's box until he either drew a walk or struck out.

I gave him all the encouragement I could. I was so convinced that Jon was unskilled and utterly lacking in talent that I continually tried to encourage him. I was constantly trying to "pump" him up.

Finally, after someone who knew something about baseball advised me that it might be more effective to coach Jon to simply watch the ball coming, instead of being told to "kill it," I realized that Jon probably already had all the tools he needed to succeed. I decided to stop letting my fears get in the way of his development.

When I did, he began playing much better baseball. I remember his first hit. As he reached second base on a double, he was literally jumping up and down while grinning at me. Despite my worries, Jon became a very good baseball player.

### Successful people make a habit of success

In considering a change in your life, refuse to allow yourself the excuse that you cannot succeed. In addition to already having the wisdom and intelligence you need, we all have the opportunity to gain success by simply *making a habit out of doing what others don't want to do.*

Consider Walt Stack, who started running when he was fifty-eight. Walt was an early leader of the fitness movement. Every morning, he could be seen running bare-chested across the Golden Gate Bridge in his bright red baseball cap. His grueling exercise regimen became a local legend.

I became aware of Walt when he finished the Ironman Triathlon in Hawaii when he was over seventy years old. It took him twenty-six hours. The next year, the Ironman instituted the "Walt Stack rule," which says the triathlon must be completed on the same day it's started.

Walt's routine was extreme. Even into his eighties, he started his day at dawn with a six-mile bike ride to the Dolphin Swim and Boat Club. From there, he jogged across the Golden Gate Bridge to Sausalito and back, about seventeen miles. Next, he swam in the bay for a half-hour in water he called "as cold as a landlord's heart." After swimming, he hopped in the sauna, sweated for a while, and then rode his bike home.

Even though he started running at close to sixty, Walt ran over 150 full-length marathons, fifteen 50-mile races and three 100-mile endurance races. He completed the Western States 100-mile endurance run and Hawaii's Ironman Triathlon after turning seventy. He ran the arduous Pike's Peak marathon, which includes a 7500-foot climb.

Stack said, "Running is habit more than anything else; you get into the habit and, if you are motivated, you find you can do a lot of things."

## Successful people form the habit of doing things unsuccessful people don't like to do.

People who thrive do what others don't want to do, don't like to do, or choose not to do.

Budd Parsons, a close friend, was built like an Olympic swimmer well into his seventies. He was about forty years my senior. We worked out at the gym and often had breakfast together. One morning I asked him about his breakfast. I had ordered ham and eggs, toast, hash browns, coffee, fruit and milk while he had oatmeal and black coffee.

The sacrifices you make today contribute to your successes tomorrow

"It looks pretty healthy," I commented. "Do you like it?" He laughed and replied, "I do now, but at first I didn't. I called it my gruel." He had learned that, to keep as fit as he liked, he had to form the habit of eating this not-too-enticing breakfast. He said it had to be a habit and that, if his mind wasn't already made up by the time he ordered his breakfast, he would probably order a strawberry waffle with a side of bacon and eggs.

He had formed the *habit* of making the decision well ahead of the point of the decision, and by forming the habit and making the decision ahead of time, he was able to eat a breakfast that contributed to his health and longevity. What was once unpleasant to him became a beloved ritual.

When we make a habit of doing things that are beneficial but we don't necessarily like, we give ourselves an edge over all the others not willing to make the same sacrifice.

## Summary

One of the strongest motivating forces known to humankind is the need to be right.

It is helpful to realize that ours was a good choice at the time we made it, with the information we had; but the information and times have changed.

The great need to be right is what stops many of us from changing.

Consider difficult people the greatest gift you have received that day, because they are teaching you something valuable.

We are bound to keep following our own mess until we get it right.

When we worry, we are visualizing that which we hope will not occur.

Successful people form the habit of doing things unsuccessful people don't like to do.

# Stage Four: Exploring

In the fourth stage, we begin to explore other possibilities and the consequences of each. "What would it be like if we moved?" "Would I be happier if I made less money but worked at a job I loved?" "How would I feel if I were married instead of single?" "Now that my mother has died, how would it feel if we were to sell her house?" "How stressful would it be if I started my own business?"

At stage four, we might seek a role model who has gone through a similar change and is enjoying a happier life. In this stage, alternatives are visualized and contemplated, signaling a deeper acceptance of the change that has already begun.

### Make your plans as fantastic as you like because 25 years from now they will seem mediocre

When we're getting ready to set off on a new adventure – and in the **Exploring** stage we're about ready to embark – it helps to have an idea about where we want to end up.

As you contemplate change and set new goals, be expansive; be visionary. One of the wealthiest people in history, Malcom Forbes, wrote:

> Make your plans as fantastic as you like, because twenty-five years from now, they will seem mediocre. Make your plans ten times as great as you first planned, in twenty-five years from now, you will wonder why you didn't make them fifty times as great.

A very successful industrial billionaire, who had prospered beyond most people's wildest imaginations, told a friend of mine, "If I had put my mind to it, I could have really achieved something."

I am convinced that most of us underrate our own capacity for achievement.

In 1969, *The Peter Principle* by Laurence Peters was published. Peters said that all of us elevate to our own level of incompetence. This, he explained, is the reason there is so much chaos and disarray, so many bureaucrats and bureaucracies. Everyone has progressed beyond the last level of his or her own competence.

When I read the book, I resisted that theme. The more I continued to think about it and the more I worked with people, it struck me that the "Peter Principle" was inconsistent with what I believed. From my observations in a career of working with business people and organizations, I offer a different principle:

### Most people haven't surpassed their own level of competency; they have simply chosen to stop progressing.

They no longer try to learn, to grow, or to stretch. This is not due to inability or low IQ: it's a choice.

What are your most "outrageous" goals?

What happens to many of us is that we become bored. We simply go home, pull the drapes, and wait for it to get late. We don't find much to motivate us, much to work toward, or much reason to improve. We end up going through the motions.

We can continue to grow until the day we die if we choose to do so. Walt Stack, the runner I mentioned in the last chapter, continued to run, bike and swim until he passed away at age eighty-six.

I suggest we set those outrageous goals Forbes wrote about and accept the task of stretching to achieve them.

There is great satisfaction in knowing that you have become all that you could have become, that you have used your life to achieve something worthwhile to you. Whatever we are doing, we are trading our time for it. It's horrible to find that you have exchanged your time – and therefore your life – for something less than it's worth.

### What skeet shooting and Lucky McDaniels taught me about goal-setting

As we begin to **Explore**, we also begin to think about setting goals. No one has ever taught me more about goal setting than Lucky McDaniels.

I met Lucky McDaniels years ago, after I discovered that I liked to shoot guns, though I had absolutely no interest in killing anything.

I especially enjoyed shotguns and what they call "big bore" guns. I learned how to reload shotgun shells and had a number of good skeet and trap guns. I enjoyed the discipline and precision it took to reload big bore: re-sizing the 30-06 casings and .45 caliber bullets, loading a new primer, getting the exact load of gunpowder into the bullet casing, and putting the new bullet in the casing.

Despite my enthusiasm, I realized that I wasn't very good at hitting the clay birds used in skeet shooting.

I decided to take a class from Lucky McDaniels, a legendary shooting instructor. McDaniels had taught the Army how to "snap shoot" in jungle fighting and had even given shooting lessons to former U.S. presidents.

During our first session, Lucky took five clay pigeons in one hand and an unplugged Remington 1100 semi-automatic skeet shotgun in the other. He threw the five clay pigeons into the air and broke them all with five separate shots before they hit the ground. Because he had thrown the clay pigeons with his left hand, they had not gone in the air very far. I was impressed.

Lucky McDaniels had some simple lessons for shooting:

1. Keep both eyes open
2. Keep both eyes on the target
3. Don't look at anything on the periphery
4. Don't get hung up on the sights on the barrel of the shotgun
5. Don't get hung up on *anything* between you and the target

After my sessions with Lucky, I couldn't wait to get back on the skeet range. I went from breaking fourteen or fifteen out of 25 clay pigeons to breaking all twenty-five – a perfect round.

When the manager of the skeet range heard about my accomplishment, he presented me with a shoulder patch. It was one of the proudest victories of my life. It wasn't because I had become such a great shot, but because I was able to follow instructions, to accept the teachings of Lucky McDaniels, and to implement them successfully.

His lessons for target shooting are also what goal setting is all about. I learned that I can hit almost any target when I keep my eyes open and focus on it.

My accomplishment was not so grand. These lessons are so simple, that even young children can learn them. When our three children were still pre-teenagers, ages 10 to 13, I took them out to teach them how to shoot.

On our first outing, I threw the disk, which was about two inches in diameter, into the air a couple of times. Each of our children shot a little under the metal disk. I instructed them as Lucky McDanielsinstructed me , *"Keep both eyes on the target."*

By concentrating on the disk, we could see the BB passing under it. Within a few more shots, each one hit the disk in the air.

Sherry, our oldest daughter became an excellent shot, as did her sister, Cynthia. They followed instructions and could hit that disk with the BB gun, ten, fifteen feet in the air every time. Their little brother Jon was equally enthusiastic about following directions, and later was able to do the same with a .410 shotgun, and then a larger shotgun.

As great a shooter as Lucky McDaniels was, I determined I could even shoot better – provided Lucky had both eyes blindfolded! Just as the principles of good shooting Lucky McDaniels taught me relate perfectly to what I know about goal-setting, so does the idea that, without goals and objectives, we are no more effective than a blindfolded shooter, no matter how expert he or she may be.

**Know what you're aiming for. When we don't set our goals or have clear-cut objectives, we are blindfolding ourselves.**

### *Effective goals are tied to results, not activities*

Many companies use what I call "management-by-drive." When sales are down, they have an enthusiastic sales drive. If expenses get out of line, they organize a drive to bring down expenses. If the accounts receivable get out line, they have a drive to collect past due accounts receivable. It's one reactive campaign after another; a ship without a port, blown by the ever-changing trade winds.

In our personal lives, too, we often do the same. Only when we get twenty pounds overweight do we take the offensive and go on a diet or begin an exercise program. This is *management-by-drive*.

In our personal and business lives, we also tend toward "management-by-exception." When a seemingly urgent crisis happens, we react to the problems that require our immediate attention, and treat them as exceptions to our overall plan. They control how we think, act, and respond. We spend our time moving from one red flag to the next. In the corporate world, this practice is sometimes called "fire drills."

Both management-by-drive and management-by-exception are examples of activity-oriented goal setting. A far better alternative is to establish clear-cut goals and then plan a set direction to achieve those objectives. *Keep your eye on the target and keep both eyes open.*

When you do this, you shift from being activity-oriented to being *results-oriented*. Many people seem to take great pride in the number of hours they work or the amount of activity they generate rather than the results they achieve. I would rather look at what I've *accomplished*.

I often ask my clients the question, "Do you have written objectives?" The answer is almost invariably, "No," or "I did once, but not now."

When I ask why not, I receive all kinds of responses, such as:

- "Every goal requires a decision, and I can't decide."

- "Goals are too limiting; they restrict us. If I don't have goals, I won't limit myself.

- "I really like to have the freedom to be spontaneous."

- "Everything is a result of chance; I don't have anything to do with the outcome."

- "No, I tried it once, but I simply lost interest."

- "Life is like a buffet line. I don't want to fill up my plate too soon. There are so many things to do, see, and accomplish. I don't want to exclude any future possibilities."

It's better to have a goal that you can change later than to have no goal at all. And even if you achieve your goal and are not completely satisfied, it's still much better than achieving nothing at all.

### Set goals, or serve someone else's

One of the pleasures of setting your own goals is that they allow you to determine your own agenda. If you don't set your own goals, someone else will, especially in times of change.

One Saturday morning, I was home watching our young children. We had lived in this new home for about three months. I was looking for something in the family room and I came across a scrapbook. Looking through the scrapbook, I saw pictures from magazines of our patio, our bedroom, and many pictures of our dining room, living room, and kitchen. I realized that it was my wife's scrapbook and we were living in *her* house. When we moved in, I had gladly left the interior design objectives completely up to her; and she did an outstanding job. If I wanted a say in the interior design of our home, it would be important for me to participate in the planning and setting of objectives.

This is true in all areas of our lives. If we want to influence the outcome, we get involved in the planning.

### One of the great joys in life is to risk failure

Some people never succeed because they don't want to fail. They live their lives on the kiddie roller coaster, never climbing very high, but never experiencing the dips either. But after you loop around the kiddie roller coaster a few times, it gets pretty boring.

It has been said the best way to succeed is to double your rate of failure. Each time you risk failure, you also risk the possibility of success. When you cease to risk failure, you often find a comfortable niche to settle into, which with a little imagination is not very different than a coffin.

*If you are not failing, you are not trying*

In my life, I have gone through flat periods in which I have been ineffective and unsatisfied. When I have been mired in these periods, it is because I have engaged only in *what I like to do* or the *urgent*, not what is most important to reach my goals.

Sustaining interest in the objective and keeping the interest alive and healthy is in itself an objective. I've found that it has taken me at least two, three, or four attempts to achieve anything of value.

Once, in an executive program at Seattle University, we read the Book of Job in the Old Testament and the Book of Romans in the New Testament and discussed them from a management and leadership point of view. This was so valuable that I set a personal goal of reading the Bible from cover to cover. A friend gave me a study guide that scheduled the reading over the course of a year. I started reading the Bible on January 1 and finished it on September 19. But I wasn't three months early. I finished it on September 19 nine years after I started. I had failed eight times!

Losing interest is not final. Sometimes you need to rediscover your internal motivation. I've mentioned a couple of times in this book that I became a charter boat captain as an avocation. What I haven't mentioned is that I failed the U.S. Coast Guard examination three times.

In the pursuit of my goals, I've found that at least one failure is about par for me. Because I know about goal setting, I also realize that if I stay focused, I will ultimately succeed; it just might take longer.

People sometimes view *setting objectives* like they're eyeing a big buffet. First, the roast leg of lamb tempts them. But before they take any, the prawns catch their attention. While they are looking at the prawns, they spy the king crab legs; but before they indulge in those, the beef tenderloin draws them away. By the time they get to the end of the line, their plate is still empty.

Rather than risk coming up with an empty plate, it's better to decide on something that will sustain us, until we can more firmly establish in our mind precisely what we want.

One of the great joys in life is to risk failure. I prefer not to fail in my personal goals, but I realize that a fear of failure results mostly because my ego is at stake.

**If we risk failure and for some reason we don't achieve our objective, our life is still enriched by our attempt.**

### How to set goals and stay on course

In the **Exploring** stage of change, we are moving away from looking at the unsatisfactory way things are to contemplation of the way we'd like them to be. In this stage, setting goals and objectives becomes vital to our later success because it concentrates our energy in the direction we want to move, and it gives us a way to stay on course.

When we establish objectives, we give ourselves the golden gift of the ability to measure our *performance*. If we know where we are going and what we want our outcome to be, it is possible to gauge our daily and weekly progress toward our desired result.

Objectives also help us measure *drift*. When you plot a course in a boat, the wind, the tides, and the currents affect how well you stay on track. Objectives show us how far off course we have drifted and aid us in making decisions. A sign in my office that I often consult reads, "Will what I am about to do help us reach our objectives?"[*]

"You must have a port of destination"

**Hans Selye**. *Author of over one- hundred books and articles on the subject of stress, summarizing his work*

When we know where we are going, it's substantially easier to make the right decisions. As I have observed earlier, advancing towards a goal provides a sense of security and reduces our stress and unhappiness. Therefore, knowing where we are headed allows us to advance, which in turns helps us to feel secure in our lives. Even if we are flat broke, making progress toward a goal gives us strength.

## Once we decide to change, our bonus is a feeling of self-worth and a sense of well-being.

When you set your goals, establish them in each major area of your life.

Here are examples:

---

[*]From the book, *Up the Organization* by Robert Townsend.

- **Domestic:** It's important to have consensus between partners. What do we want to accomplish at home? How do we spend our discretionary time? How do we spend our discretionary income? Where do we want to live? What should our home look like inside and outside? What can we do to build our relationship? How will we parent our children?

- **Career:** Where do I want to be five years from now? Ten years from now? What do I want to accomplish? What do I want to be remembered for? What steps do I have to take? With whom do I need to interact?

- **Health:** Do I want to lose weight? Gain weight? Do I want to exercise? Do I like group activities or do I prefer to work out at home? Do I need a workout buddy?

- **Spiritual:** For some people, spiritual goals are defined best in terms of what they want to be involved in. Church? Spiritual group? Do I want to read spiritual books? What do I want to listen to?

- **Social:** What do I want to do in my community? My neighborhood? What organizations do I want to join? Who will my friends be?

- **Financial:** This area is probably the easiest for most of us to define. How much do I want to earn? Invest? What am I willing to give up to reach my financial goals? What do I want to own? How important is vacation? What "toys" do I want? How much will I need in savings when I retire?

- **Intellectual:** What do I want to learn? What educational courses? What tapes? What books? What study groups? How do I want to grow intellectually?

When you honor your commitments over your preference of the moment, when you choose to do what you said solely because you said so, in that moment you are expressing yourself as action, rather than as a collection of mere ideas, wishes or dreams.

**Werner Erhard**

Set quantitative, measurable goals. If your goal can't be described numerically, be as definitive as possible so that you can easily measure your progress.

Study your goals. It helps to discuss them with someone close to you.

Next, *write them down*. Remember to be as clear and specific as you can. Your plans may not work out exactly as you had hoped; or, they may work out far better than you had imagined. But unless you write them down, you are not likely to get what you want. Let me repeat that, because it is important:

## You increase the odds of reaching your goals when you write them down.

Writing down your goals is like planting a seed in the fertile garden of your mind. When that seed germinates in your inner mind, the battle is half won, because the inner mind works both night and day.

Dr. Maxwell Maltz, creator of the self-improvement phenomenon Psycho-Cybernetics, hypothesized that when we write our goals down, we link our brain and nervous system together in the same pursuit. They combine much like the mechanical and computer parts of a heat-seeking missile, which work together to guide it toward its target.

Using a tape recorder, tape your goals and listen to them until you have burned them into your mind.

Make visuals. Go to an art or business supply store and get a 30" x 36" poster board or use a scrapbook. Make a display, something you can see, hold and feel. Pictures will reinforce and remind you of your goals.

Determine the specific action steps necessary to accomplish your objectives. Outline the steps in chronological order with the most important first (not the easiest).

Keep a journal in your desk. Instead of using it for writing the complaints, the problems and the challenges of the day, write about your experiences and your progress toward reaching your objectives. Write daily: What are you experiencing? What have you found supportive? What have you accomplished?

Writing a journal keeps you accountable and increases your motivation.

Let's look at how setting a goal guides your decisions and helps you stay on course: A client of mine was on vacation with his wife and two teenage boys. It was the week between Christmas and New Year's. While their two teenage sons played in the snow, my client and his wife went shopping and found themselves in a beautiful shop in the village. Because it was the end of the calendar year, the shop had marked down their full-length leather coats to half price.

For years, my client had casually thought about owning a full-length leather coat and, at fifty percent off, they were enticing. The coat was on sale for $400 and his wife suggested he buy it. He put on the coat and examined himself in the mirror. It fit perfectly. Temptation set in.

But then, he thought back to our conversations about his goals. He had determined that he wanted to retire at age fifty-five, spend 15 percent of his time writing, speak to civic groups three times a year, and travel eight weeks a year. He also thought about the boat he wanted and the many other objectives he had set for his retirement.

Although the coat was only $400, he asked himself, "Will what I'm about to do take me closer to my objectives?"

It took him less than a minute to reach the decision, "No!" He decided that the cost would not help him in his professional life or bring him closer to his goal of retiring at fifty-five; so, he chose not to buy it.

And yes, he did retire at fifty-five, and yes, he wrote and, as a matter of fact, he dedicated his first book to me. It was one of the greatest honors of my lifetime.

### Create the picture in your mind

Harold Sherman and Claude Bristol wrote *TNT: The Power Within You*, one of the earliest books on goal setting.[†]

I met and spent time with Harold, discussing many of his ideas. He believed that we must create a clear picture of what we want in our minds and, because the creative power of the subconscious does not reason, we can create anything we can imagine. When we know what we want, we must not let doubt creep in to change the picture.

**If you can develop a burning desire for what you want, you will experience one of the great motivating forces in our life.**

---

[†] Harold later re-wrote and re-titled it *The New TNT*.

Harold went on to insist that we visualize what we want: get a picture, make a model or, if possible, *act it out*. To illustrate his point, he told a story about Liberace.

Liberace took the theories of Sherman and Bristol to heart. He relaxed, created a picture of what he wanted in his mind, and turned his thoughts to how to achieve it.

Liberace wanted to perform to a sold-out concert in the Hollywood Bowl, one of the premiere concert venues of the time. So he rented a piano and trucked it to the Hollywood Bowl when it was empty. He paid the manager and the security personnel some walking around money and had the piano moved onto the stage. Liberace then stood on the stage, bowed to his imaginary audience, and played to the vast deserted Bowl. He addressed the sold-out audience he imagined, and pictured himself receiving a standing ovation. Anyone observing this scene might have thought Liberace a little deranged.

Four years later, he reached his seemingly improbable goal. Liberace performed a concert in the Hollywood Bowl to a packed house and received a standing ovation. The reviews of the concert claimed it was a brilliant performance. Next came television, Las Vegas, and the fame that he had pictured for himself.

It takes courage and effort to *act out* our goals like that. I ask myself sometimes, "Have I become too 'sophisticated' to take those steps? Am I willing to do something like that for my goals?"

Years after Harold told me that story, I had an assistant, Dave, who worked with me in a seminar. Dave was one of the finest persons I have ever met. He was somewhat shy, very sincere, but not particularly verbal.

During the morning session of the seminar, I spoke about Harold Sherman and told the Liberace story. After we broke for lunch, I went back to the room to prepare for the afternoon session.

Dave was already there. As I entered the room from a door perpendicular to the lectern, Dave did not hear me enter into the carpeted room. I saw him looking down from the lectern speaking to an imaginary audience, and I realized he was visualizing his future as a speaker. After a moment, I let him know that I was in the room. He wasn't embarrassed at all. He looked over at me and smiled. He knew what he was doing; I knew what he was doing; and, at that moment, we bonded.

Dave did not fit the physical profile that some expect of the average speaker or seminar leader. Yet, while he worked at a paper company, he became an excellent presenter by:

- Forming the picture
- Writing out his goal
- Putting on the appearance of success

He spoke to art groups, printing groups, graphic artists, designers, just about anyone who used large quantities of paper. Dave developed into an interesting, informative and inspiring speaker. Until his retirement, he had an excellent career speaking to groups around the Northwest.

### Find the reason why

My running companion's grandmother was in her seventies when she was diagnosed with cancer. At the time, my running companion was a sophomore in high school. His grandmother's life ambition at that point was to see the first person in their family graduate from high school. She became obsessed with watching her grandson graduate. She lived another two years to see it. The day after he graduated, she died.

Viktor Frankl, who survived four death camps during World War II, wrote *Man's Search for Meaning*, an engrossing description of his experiences. Frankl said that simply finding the will to live was too much for many people in the death camps. The utter horror of the reality in which they found themselves made death preferable to life.

In order to keep up the will to survive, Frankl found people needed something to live for, a *why*. Whether it was to see loved ones again or avenge the crimes done to them, Frankl found that when people have a reason *why*, they can usually find the *how* to do anything.

Frankl's original *why* was to live to see his wife again. When he found out she had died in another camp, his reason *why* changed. His *why* became to survive so that he could finish the manuscript he planned to write about the horrible experiences in the camp. Originally titled *From Death Camp to Existentialism*, Frankl's book, *Man's Search for Meaning*, became a worldwide bestseller.

Few things are as powerful as discovering the why. If you know the why, you have the key to know how to do just about anything in any circumstance.

Let me give you a powerful example from my own life.

In high school, I had a close friend named Fred. He and I were more interested in drinking, playing pool, and having fun than we were in our studies. He was a great buddy and I enjoyed spending time with him.

After high school, when the Korean War began, I joined the Navy and Fred became a Marine. Fred was captured during battle and placed in a POW camp in North Korea. He escaped four times and was re-captured three. Each time, he was returned to the camp, placed in isolation, tortured, beaten and starved. After he was returned to the general prison population, he spent every waking hour plotting his next escape.

I was stationed in Guam in the South Pacific, when Fred finally escaped the fourth and final time and made it to freedom. When Fred returned to our hometown, our largest newspaper started a series about him with a front-page article. It chronicled his capture, his confinement and his escape. It told of how he pulled out an abscessed tooth with pliers and no anesthesia, and graphically portrayed other hardships he had endured. It detailed each of his escapes and ultimate captures. The article revealed his creativeness, his resourcefulness and his great courage.

I couldn't wait to get back to the States to see Fred. Unfortunately, his story had not ended. When he returned home, he found that his fiancée, one of the most strikingly beautiful women either of us had ever known, had fallen in love with and married someone else. She had assumed that he had been killed in the war.

What kept Fred going through his POW experiences, his why, was the picture he held in his mind of returning home to the woman he loved.

One of the first things Fred did when he came home was to purchase a new Corvette. Within a week, he crashed the car into a telephone pole at high speed and was killed.

I've often wondered how someone could survive all that Fred did and then die so tragically. Since Viktor Frankl introduced me to the need to have a reason "why," I have encountered many similarly poignant stories about people who have endured great difficulties, and then, when the reason "why" no longer existed, had it all fall apart.

## Deliver the body

I once had the opportunity to ask Earl Willets, a legendary fitness trainer, what he had learned in his profession. He told me that achieving personal fitness is the same as achieving any other goal.

The first step is to set an objective, and then determine the reason why you want to achieve it and the way you will do it. If the goal is to improve physically, then a person should set a workout schedule to achieve that objective.

I asked him what he had observed in the gym, what happened when a person was too tired from work, or simply too wiped out from being out late the night before if they were on an early morning schedule. He told me that people who achieve their goals bring a stool into the gym when they feel under the weather and watch the other people in the room work out. While they might not be up to it that day, they don't want to interrupt the habit of going to the gym.

They "deliver the body" on the days they feel too tired. Even if they don't feel up to working out, they maintain the habit of going to the gym. Those who do not "deliver the body" interrupt that habit, and often do not start again.

Deliver your body, and your mind will follow

## Work hard, but work smart

I have always encouraged clients – and myself – to work hard. Successful, effective people do work hard. But I'm convinced that it is much more important to have clear-cut objectives.

We must be very aware of the possibility that our work is becoming more important than our objectives. When we disappear into our duties, we lose sight of what we hope to accomplish beyond the hours we put in each week. Our objectives become submerged under our activity.

I learned at an early age that hard work does not get you everywhere. When I was a young man, I worked in a lumber mill, "pulling on the green chain." As the green logs came out of the holding pond and started up into the mill toward the sawyer (the person who operates the saws), they were extremely wet and heavy. The logs were sent down through the saws and cut into two-by-eights and two-by-tens. These pieces of lumber came out onto the green chain, where I picked up and stacked the timber before it was lifted up by a forklift and taken to a kiln to be dried.

It was one of the hardest physical jobs in the West. The pay was good for the lumber mill, but I quickly learned that hard work alone was not going to make me successful, nor would it provide what I wanted for my family.

If you dedicate yourself to working hard, make sure you are working toward your goals. Recall the lesson: put what you want into a visual picture and spend fifteen minutes in the morning and night visualizing it.

**When you have a clear goal and a reason why you want to achieve it, you will figure out how to do it.**

### How to avoid creative avoidance

Some years ago, I started running to develop my health and strengthen my heart and cardiovascular system. At first, the experience was unpleasant and I disliked it.

I began to have injury after injury. In sequence, my injuries included my right calf, my left foot, my thigh, my lower back, my Achilles tendon, and then my left calf. Every time I experienced an injury, I stopped running until it healed. I finally realized these injuries were my way of avoiding running, which I disliked. I was *psychosomatically* inducing my injuries, pain, and discomfort.

At one point, I put my hand down on my right Achilles tendon and could feel the little bubble where it was inflamed. I simply affirmed, "I choose to run and no longer avoid this, I release this pain," and stopped running until it healed.

I discussed my injuries with a doctor and he indicated that if I was going to run, I would have to start stretching. I started stretching for about fifteen minutes before every run; the foot, calf, hamstring, quadriceps, thigh, back, and especially the Achilles tendon. The Achilles tendon no longer gave me problems.

> The mind will often go to great lengths to protect us from the effects of change

I then started studying the subject of creative avoidance. I found that if I wanted to avoid something, I would harness my conscious mind (and my subconscious mind as well, I'm certain), and become very creative in finding ways to avoid whatever it was. I discovered that as I experience change, my mind goes to great lengths to protect me from something that is unpleasant, such as running.

The 19th century British historian, Lord Acton, famously observed, "Power corrupts, and absolute power corrupts absolutely." It's worth noting that the **lack** of power also corrupts. When people feel powerless, they become self-absorbed and attempt to gain control. This is as true in family and social relationships as it is in work environments.

> Powerlessness corrupts

As we clarify our options in the **Exploring** stage of change, and create more fully realized visualizations of where we are headed, we may encounter a new kind of resistance from within that comes from a sense of powerlessness. This particular resistance, *creative avoidance*, often appears to have origins outside of us, but actually is something we ourselves create.

In essence, creative avoidance is what we do to avoid having to deal with a change. We procrastinate, find excuses, or even make ourselves ill to get out of facing the unknown or what we fear may be unpleasant.

## Making ourselves ill is actually a natural way to protect against the stresses of change.

Dr. Thomas Holmes, when he headed the department of psychiatry at the University of Washington in the early 1950s, noticed that tuberculosis had occurred among patients after a cluster of disruptive events, such as a death in the family, a new job, or a marriage. He came up with what he referred to as the "mother-in-law syndrome".[‡] He wrote, "A person often catches a cold when a mother-in-law comes to visit. Patients mentioned mothers-in-law so often that we came to consider them a common cause of disease in the United States."

Rather than pick on mother-in-laws, I would probably refer to it as the father-in-law syndrome; the fact that I am one seems to make that more acceptable.

Dr. Holmes did research on the impact of "life change" events and wrote that he could even induce the symptoms brought on by the "in-law syndrome" as he interviewed students and others.

He would be talking to them about what led up to their coming down with a cold or the flu, and even though they were then totally recovered, just by talking about the impending visit of someone who really distressed them,

---

[‡] Not politically correct today.

the individual would start to exhibit a runny nose, begin coughing, and show signs of fever.

I have seen this syndrome in a bright and successful young client of mine. She explained that while attending a wedding, her mother-in-law spoke negatively and severely with her. The mother-in-law had cornered my client at the reception and shared her critical opinions of her.

My client said that even though she had gone to the wedding feeling wonderful, after the encounter with her mother-in-law, she felt all of the symptoms of a cold. By the time she and her husband reached home, she was ill. She had a high fever and remained ill for the better part of a week.

It's important to understand that creative avoidance actually stops us from changing or reaching our goals. It leads us to avoid our fears rather than face them.

I once made a dear friend very angry with me when I pointed out his own creative avoidance.

My close friend, Lew Hopkins (a general contractor) and I owned a boat together that we used to sport fish salmon. Even though it was moored on the Pacific Ocean, neither of us had ever been more than ten or fifteen miles offshore.

Lew had a dream to sail from California to Hawaii and on to Tahiti. He bought a 42-foot sailboat and moored it in Newport Beach, California. He lived aboard the sailboat and devoted himself to learning the necessary skills to pilot a craft across the ocean.

After he had been in Newport Beach for about six months, Lew called me. I asked him how his trip to Hawaii was progressing and he said he was learning to use the sextant.

A few months later, he called again. I asked when he was leaving for Hawaii. He said he had ordered a

LORAN, a long-range navigational instrument, and needed to become more proficient on the sextant to shoot the sun and stars in order to find his position in the event his LORAN malfunctioned. I asked him how long that would take and he figured about another month.

Three months later, he called again, still in Newport Beach. He said he had learned the sextant and had installed the LORAN but his three-member crew had become tired of waiting and left, and it would take a while to find another crew.

Three months after that, we were visiting on the phone and I again asked him when he was leaving. He said he had a little bit of pain down his left arm and in his chest, and he was going through a series of tests to have his heart checked out to see if it was angina.

Shortly after that, Lew came up to Seattle and we went to dinner. I gently asked him if there was a possibility that he was creatively avoiding this marvelous adventure, his trip to Hawaii and Tahiti.

Lew became visibly upset with me.

I explained that I had creatively avoided my own success in a rather dramatic fashion and told Lew about the first marathon I ran.

I hadn't run at all during my youth and had begun running seriously only in my early forties. The marathon was scheduled for the first Saturday after Thanksgiving. A week before the big day, I set out on a planned 22-mile run. About five and a half miles into the run, I was working up a small hill when there was an explosion in my lower back. The sudden pain was so sharp that I actually fell and skinned my hands and knees.

I got up, and slowly hobbled the short distance to our home. It was a Sunday morning and our teenage son was home. He took me to the emergency room of the nearest hospital and the X-rays showed no structural damage.

Without an MRI or dye test, they couldn't really tell if there was anything seriously wrong with a disk or the spine, but the doctor ventured that it was a muscle spasm.

He ordered me to bed and prescribed muscle relaxants. I went on to tell Lew that I had stayed in bed on Sunday and Monday and kept thinking, "What about my first marathon would cause me to bring this injury on? Was it self-induced?"

It didn't take long to figure out that I was afraid of this run. I was afraid that I was too old, too slow, that I would fail, and that people would find out that I just didn't have what it takes to finish a marathon. People would find out that I was phony, that I could talk it and I could train it but I couldn't do it. It's amazing how the mind creates a pitch-black negative picture if you allow it.

As I lay in bed for two days, it occurred to me that if I brought this on, if I self-induced the muscle spasm, I could accelerate the healing. I could figure out how to extricate myself from the pain, the discomfort, and certainly from the fear of failure.

I started affirming my health, my recovery and my healing.

On Tuesday, approximately forty-eight hours after I fell, I was up and walking. That morning, I did a stand-up seminar aided with a tall stool I used to rest on periodically.

On Wednesday, I shuffled, walked and trotted about a half-mile. On Thursday, Thanksgiving Day, I walked, shuffled, and ran about one mile before dinner. On Friday, I shuffled, walked, and ran about three miles.

Much of the pain and discomfort were gone.

On the Saturday after Thanksgiving, I arrived for my first marathon. The temperature was 38 degrees; it was raining steadily and the wind was blowing. Finally, after standing around waiting, the marathon got underway. For the first ten miles, I kept thinking that my back would blow out again. I had the fear of the pain coming back, the fear of failure, the fear of not making it.

Then the thought occurred to me that probably never in the history of that marathon or any other marathon have they ever lost anyone on the course. There are marvelous volunteers, aid cars, aid stations and countless other runners. Someone would see me go down, call for assistance, rescue me, and take me to an emergency room.

That relieved my mind completely and I started running without apprehension.

But our minds work in strange ways. I started hoping that perhaps I would go down; it would be a way of getting away from this bitter cold, wind and rain. Going down would end this terrible discomfort.

Over our dinner, I told Lew that I worked my way through all these fears and negative thoughts and finally finished the marathon.

I told Lew that I had become so wonderfully creative in avoiding that undertaking that I almost creatively avoided my way out of what turned out to be a great experience.

I had structured it so that no one could criticize me. They would say: "After all, he couldn't run, his back went out. He was in the emergency room just six days before the run, what do you expect?" Subconsciously and consciously, I was covered.

I ended my story by telling Lew, who had by now calmed down, that I completed my first marathon in four hours and five minutes, which isn't real fast but a major victory nonetheless.

When we left each other after dinner, there was nothing further said about creative avoidance or his proposed sailing trip. I didn't hear from Lew for about another three months.

Then I got a call on a Thursday night.

I couldn't resist asking him, "Where are you, Lew?"

He said, "I just called to tell you that I'm doing fine."

"Where are you?" I repeated.

He said, "I'm calling you from a payphone on the dock at the yacht club in Honolulu."

I don't remember much of the rest of that conversation except that I was so overwhelmed that I probably got a little dewy-eyed as I was listening to him tell me about his trip.

It was a great victory for Lew, a victory over self and over creative avoidance.

He closed with some words that have stuck with me. He said he had become very angry and defensive after I had told him he might be creatively avoiding his trip. He said he couldn't get it out of his mind all the way back to California, and for the next few days, he pondered it and realized that it was true.

He said: "I wish you had laid your rap on me years ago, but *whenever we want to learn, the teacher appears*." He went on to explain that he had creatively avoided so many things throughout his life that he had learned how to set it up to make it look OK to fail. He said it was time for him to face life, do his best, and not concern himself as much with the outcome as with the trying.

Resist the impulse to avoid your own adventure

Lew fully realized his great adventure, sailing from Hawaii to Tahiti. He stayed at Papeete, sailed back to Hawaii and later sold his boat and flew back to the mainland. He later said that facing his fears in order to make the voyage was the greatest victory of his life,

## Summary

Most people haven't surpassed their own level of competency; they have simply chosen to stop progressing.

When we don't set our goals or have clear-cut objectives, we are blindfolding ourselves.

If we risk failure and for some reason we don't achieve our objective, our life is enriched by our attempt.

Once we decide to change, our bonus is a feeling of self-worth and a sense of well-being.

You increase the odds of reaching your goals when you write them down.

Develop a burning desire for what you want and experience one of the great motivating forces in our life.

When you have a clear goal and a reason why you want to achieve it, you will figure out how to do it.

The best way to succeed at what we choose is to study what those who have gone before us have done and learn from them the steps they have taken.

Making ourselves ill is a natural way to protect against the stresses of change.

# Stage Five: Experimenting

In this stage, the alternatives we contemplated are tested in various ways. When we reach this stage, we are completely thawed out and our icy reluctance to change is replaced by an increasing desire to "get on with it." Still, because we are unsure of where we heading, we will go through a period of testing. Some couples choose to live together before they commit to marriage. People like to test-drive a car before they buy it. Someone might visit the foreign city in which they have a new job offer to see how it feels. While experimenting, we have a great opportunity to learn from others. The greater someone might fear a change, the longer this period might be. The experimental stage is a sign that change is around the corner.

### *The importance of self-image in change*

There is a story, possibly apocryphal, about a railroad employee who constantly heard warnings about the dangers of getting locked in a refrigerator car and freezing to death. One day, when he was working alone in just such a car, the door swung closed and latched on the outside, locking him in. He banged, shouted and hollered until he became exhausted. He heard a loud humming sound from outside and knew that the refrigeration unit in his car was on. He felt cold, and he assumed he was going to die.

> "The mind is its own place and can make a heaven of hell and a hell of heaven."
>
> **John Milton,** *17th century poet*

Inside the car, he found a piece of chalk and began writing on the wall of the car. He recorded his experience, a full chronology of the stages of freezing to death. When his co-workers found him, he was dead. His body exhibited the signs of having frozen to death. Bizarrely, the refrigeration unit was not turned on. The temperature in the car was only in the low 40s.

The story, urban legend or not, illustrates an important truth about the power of our minds. Current brain research shows that, when we fantasize a situation, our brain doesn't assume it is fantasy. It thinks it's *real* and will cause bodily reactions consistent with the fantasized situation. This is why people sitting in a perfectly safe room will experience all the physical signs of fear just because they are watching a scary movie. Their brains react to the movie as though it were really happening.

When we are in the **Experimenting** stage, we are striving to create a new reality first in our minds and second in our lives.

It has often been observed that a baby has only two fears: loud noises and falling. All of our other fears are learned.

We *learn* the attitudes we hold, including learning that if we are locked in the refrigeration car, we will freeze to death.

The institutionalized characters in the book *One Flew Over the Cuckoo's Nest* (Ken Kesey, 1962) are examples of people who are prisoners of their own minds. One of the patients in the mental ward, Harding, admits he isn't committed, and says, "As a matter of fact, there are only a few men on the ward who *are* committed."

The main character, McMurphy (played by Jack Nicholson in the 1975 film) responds, "You gripe, you bitch for weeks on end about how you can't stand this place, can't stand the nurse or anything about her, and all the time you ain't committed. I can understand with some of those old guys on the ward. They are nuts. But you, you're not exactly the everyday man on the street, but you are not nuts."

Another inmate, Billy, joins in: "If I had the guts, I could go outside today. If I had the guts, my mother is a

"You've got to be taught/ To hate and fear,/ You've got to be taught/ From year to year,/ It's got to be drummed/ In your dear little ear/ You've got to be carefully taught."

**Oscar Hammerstein**, *South Pacific.*

good friend of Nurse Rachet, and I could get signed out this afternoon if I had the guts."

Our *self-image* largely determines whether or not we have the courage to "get signed out" of our own versions of the refrigerator car, the mental ward, the poverty, the oppressive work situation, or the unhappy relationship.

*Our self-image determines our level of success and performance*

Mary, a woman in one of my seminars, demonstrated this power. Mary was overworked and exhausted, being a single mother with four children, a full-time job as a supervisor, a second job delivering newspapers, and going to college.

During the seventh week of my seminar, she came to class with a cast on her leg that ran from ankle to thigh. When I asked what happened, she said that she had broken her kneecap in a motorcycle accident and was on sick leave until she recovered. She only came to work to sit in on my seminar. I was honored.

I asked her how she was enjoying her time off. Mary was finally getting the rest she needed. She was enjoying being able to watch soap operas on television, and read all the magazines and books piled up in her house. She said she had even taken to buying a box of chocolates to nibble on while reading and watching her soap operas. She used the word, "decadent." She was loving it. She called it, "the time of her life."

"Is there an outside chance you . . .?" I began to ask. I didn't even finish the question. We had been talking about self-image in the previous session and she answered emphatically, "absolutely yes!" cutting me off. She explained, "I needed the time off, I needed the rest, it was my way of not having a nervous breakdown or burning out."

She explained that she knew consciously and subconsciously that she needed some time off, and that she would go to any length to get it, even breaking her kneecap. That was her conclusion, not mine.

After we finished our work with her firm, Mary stayed in touch. She said that much of what she learned would make it possible for her to find balance in her life by assigning priorities, looking at her values, and creating the picture that would include perfect health and balance.

Daily, she re-formed her self-image to be able to get what she needed without breaking her own kneecap:

- I see myself getting proper rest.

- I see myself enjoying perfect health.

- I see myself with balance in my life.

- I see myself being a loving parent, always positive and encouraging.

- I see myself as a thoughtful, considerate, and caring team member on my job.


If Mary is right about why she had her accident, it suggests that we really can create any situation we want, be it positive or negative.

Altering our self-image is a significant factor for turning change into a payday, because it is through our self-image that we place limitations and draw boundaries for ourselves.

Dr. Prescott Leckey, in his book, *Self Consistency*, wrote about the role that self-image plays in individual achievement. Leckey worked with students from the inner city at Columbia University. He found that, if the students' image of themselves was inconsistent with the material, they did not learn it. Leckey found that when he changed the students' self-image, their attitude toward the material changed, and they began to learn and retain what they had learned.

Leckey tutored the students on how to spell certain words. He discovered that after a period of training, they became outstanding spellers. However, if their self-image did not include a picture of themselves as good spellers, after four or five weeks they reverted back to spelling poorly, as they had done before.

We protect ourselves from the pain of contradiction by making it seem consistent to be a poor speller, a slow reader, or whatever it is that is impacting our life. The longer we maintain the standard, the greater the handicap becomes. We become more rooted in the shortcoming, simply believing it is "part of who I am." In Leckey's research, he explained:

*My poor performance is not a part of who I am, no matter how much I want to believe that*

> We first explain to the pupils that their deficiency is not due to their lack of ability, but to a standard to which they have created for themselves. Finally, we call attention without criticism to the inconsistency between mature and immature standards. We make the conflict as clear as possible. This way, we take advantage of the *need for consistency*, and make it work in a pupil's favor instead of against them. We can influence the pupils to change their behavior in order to preserve their mental integrity, but not in order to prepare themselves to make them a material or financial success.

The key concept here is *consistency*. To find what my image of myself is, all I have to do is look around. It consistently surrounds me. It is evident in everything I choose: the carpets, the plants, the books, the lighting, the organization of my desk, the suit I'm wearing, my leisure clothes. I selected all of these items, and they all reflect part of what I am. If I change them, I expect that my actions would change to become *consistent* with my surroundings. Our actions will be harmonious with the vision we have of ourselves in our minds. In order to retain our sanity, they have to be.

*Our actions will be consistent with the vision we have of ourselves in our minds*

One of the most difficult challenges is to create an environment in which changing your self-image is possible. Many people have used the incentive of money and financial success; but if the pictures we hold of ourselves do not include success at what we are doing, any victory will be short-lived. We will see temporary gains as flukes, and return to our previous self-image.

Airplanes have an instrument called an attitude indicator in the control panel, which shows how the plane is flying in relation to the horizon. When the wings tip, the instrument displays how far off the line of the horizon the plane has deviated. People self-adjust in the same manner. When we act in a way inconsistent with our attitudes, something inside us works to bring us back in line. Over time, we can change our attitudes, and with them, the level of the "horizon."

It seems that some people consistently win, while others of equal or more ability consistently lose. Both winning and losing are the results of habitually self-adjusting the visions of ourselves that we hold in our minds.

When we establish an image in our mind, we conform to the expectations of that image because we have a need to be consistent, even if it is to consistently fail.

## It becomes just as hard to break a pattern of success as it does a pattern of failure.

**Eliminate the mindset that excuses failure**

If you eliminate the mindset that says, "It's OK to lose," then you erase the temptation to find an excuse to lose.

While playing golf, I have seen many outstanding games marred by one or two easily correctable mistakes. Those mistakes often seem intentionally committed. Every Saturday morning, week in and week out, I've seen a golfer step up to the tenth tee and pull one or two or three balls out of bounds to the left. He doesn't pull out of bounds on holes one through nine or on holes eleven to eighteen. Just the tenth hole. As they say, "That tenth hole owns him." *What is your tenth hole?*

Even more to the point, how do I get on the tenth-hole green on the first try? Dr. Maxwell Maltz wrote in his book *Psycho-Cybernetics*:

> When Ben Hogan is playing in a tournament, he mentally rehearses each shot, just before making it. He makes the shot perfectly in his imagination – 'feels' the club head strike the ball just as it should. He 'feels' himself performing the perfect following through – and then steps up to the ball, and depends upon what he calls 'muscle memory' to carry out the shot just as he has imagined it.

Dr. Maltz goes on to say, "You must have a clear mental picture of the correct thing before you can do it successfully."

Unfortunately, when we are facing a challenge, whether it is on the tenth hole or in some other area of our life, we form a "3-D" picture in our mind of what we don't want to happen. We visualize hooking the ball out of bounds, fumbling through an interview, or blowing a sales call.

So often, when we are trying to achieve something, we grit our teeth, clench our jaw, "cinch down," and compound the challenge confronting us. What Dr. Maltz is teaching us is to *relax*, form the picture of what we want to happen, and see ourselves accomplishing it.

When facing a challenge, relax and visualize success

What we do today is the result of a combination of the following.

- What we have told ourselves

- What we have listened to from others

These are the leverage points for changing our self-image.

When dealing with ourselves, we should think in positive, uplifting, and if necessary, corrective ways. This is an option that is open to all of us. My favorite affirmations, those that I would put in my pocket and read often during the day, are:

- "I have a good feeling about reaching my goals."
- "I enjoy giving compliments."
- "I feel good about myself and those whom I meet."
- "I express an attitude of gratefulness in all that I do and say."
- "I enjoy growing and learning new things from my work, the books I read and the people with whom I associate."
- "I learn from everyone that I meet."
- "I'm very happy and I enjoy life."
- "I am enjoying perfect health and for that I am grateful."

When interacting with others, we should present the image of the person we wish to be. We all put on a costume consistent with our own self-image, and people relate to us through that costume. The objective is to wear a "costume" or "uniform" consistent with what you want to be. If you are not there yet, you should still dress in a way that shows others the person how you wish to be perceived. When you do this, people react to it, and you have begun taking the steps to realize the change.

When our self-image is formed, it is stored in our subconscious, which reinforces it. Interestingly enough, the subconscious is *neutral*. It doesn't care. Whatever you feed it is exactly what it will do. You tell it to wake you at 4:00 a.m.; it doesn't worry about whether or not you've had enough sleep, it will wake you at 4:00 a.m.

*Our self-image rests in our subconscious, which is neutral. We can feed it positive or negative images.*

**If you feed your subconscious an image of success that's what you are going to get. The pictures we hold in our minds lead us in the direction we are going.**

### *Experimenting requires patience, sacrifice, and a willingness to live outside of our comfort zones*

Many of us want what we want *when* we want it. We put off our wishes until the exact moment we want them to occur.

An experiment requires patience. In the period from 1878 to 1880, the inventor Thomas Edison and his associates worked on at least *three thousand* different theories to develop an efficient incandescent lamp.

Success might not come tomorrow, next week or even next year, but if we work at it, success will come. Many brilliant persons have distinguished themselves though their perseverance. If you want prosperity next year, start visualizing, planning and acting now.

Some call this *future tripping*, but it strikes me as *present tripping*. Once we know how today fits into where we want to be next year, our decisions and actions lead us towards that end. Like bricks in a building, today fits into tomorrow, into next week, into next month. What we eat, what we spend, what we save, what we read and who we spend time with today will show up in our future.

An experiment to change your life will undoubtedly require sacrifice from you.

What are you willing to give up?

Peter Emt, an old friend of mine, believed that this question was the key to prosperity. Peter was originally from Connecticut, but he settled in the Northwest, where he bought a small ranch and feedlot. It became the heart of a town in later years; Peter obviously had insights about real estate. Peter also owned a fuel business and bought real estate, becoming affluent in the process. He was active in his church, where he attended Mass daily and served as the CEO of the Salvage Bureau, which collected clothes, toys, and other goods that were sold through a retail outlet. He was generous with both his time and his money.

Despite his wealth, Peter drove an old Army surplus jeep and wore suits, which, while immaculately pressed, were modest.

I asked him how he became so prosperous.

He told me that when he started buying real estate, he had to sacrifice some of what he wanted at the time. He couldn't buy property and have the newest car, fancy clothes, or take long vacations. He was willing to give these things up because he knew what he wanted – financial security. Peter said it's a trade off. As the highly successful basketball coach, Pat Riley wrote in his 1994 book, *The Winner Within*:

*What sacrifices would you make in order to be successful?*

## "You can have anything you want; you just can't have everything."

Be careful about what you're *not willing* to give up to achieve your dreams. Some people don't want to move, attend class after work, give up their weekends, drive a less expensive car, live in a low cost home, work out of a low overhead office, and on and on. If the things you are not willing to give up contradict your goals, you will be hindered from the success you want.

When we make sacrifices to pursue a positive change, we are catapulted out of our *comfort zone*. This brings us back to self-image. Just as we set our own self-image, we also set our own comfort levels. For example, I felt comfortable at 160 pounds. When my weight went up to 170 pounds, I became accustomed to that. I also adjusted when I reach 180 pounds. When I saw a picture of myself at 200 pounds, I realized that I had become fat.

Because I had become accustomed to the weight, losing it was extremely uncomfortable. I had to visualize myself at a lower weight and then set goals to take off the extra pounds. When I saw a slice of cheesecake being served to me, I didn't eat it, as delicious as I knew it would be, because eating it was inconsistent with my weight loss goals.

I had to develop new eating habits. After I lost the weight, the longer I kept it off, the more comfortable I became, until I *established a new comfort zone*.

When you establish a new comfort zone, it is natural to experience setbacks. A friend of mine went from 260 pounds to 170, but his picture of himself did not include his being 170. He went back up to 260. Then he changed the picture he held of himself. He affirmed himself at 170 pounds and started playing "what if." "What if I lose 90 pounds? What would it feel like to have all that energy?"

Don't think you need to change everything right away. It's OK to move at a measured pace.

If you placed a plank between two skyscrapers one thousand feet in the air, most of us would find it impossible to cross. But if you take the same plank and place it three inches above the floor, we could cross it easily. To change your comfort level, you must slowly raise the plank. Start with it at three inches above the floor and move up from there. You'll be higher than you realize before you know it.

### There is time to experiment and time to change

"We don't live long enough to take time seriously."

**George Bernard Shaw,** *Methuselah*

Experimenting with different approaches to your life – "test-driving" changes – requires time. In the midst of a life-altering event, such as death, divorce or a move, time feels scarce. When we are struggling through a change, our days can feel barely manageable, as though there's just enough time to meet the minimum threshold of our responsibilities. How then, can one possibly find the time to do the**Experimenting** stage of change justice?

I've reached the conclusion that *there is always time to do what is important.* Unfortunately, we often spend this life as though it were a practice run for the next.

We often operate in the mid-range of mediocrity. I have observed that effective achievers use small increments of time to get important things done. They think of each moment as an opportunity. Those of us who don't pay attention to their minutes are likely to take a random walk through life wasting them.

I knew that if I was going to find time to change and grow, I needed to embrace the discipline of time management. Here are strategies that worked for me:

"You must never find time for anything. If you want time you must make it."

**Charles Buxton,** *1823-1871 British author*

- I had to discipline myself to wake up early and not to stay too long in bed. When I wake up, I get up.

- I prepare for work the night before, and lay out my clothes and everything that I will need.

- I try to make the first hour of the workday my most important and productive hour.

- I started *skimming* newspapers and magazines. If I was going to stay current and have an awareness of world events, I could get most of what I needed with a fast reading and defer the detailed reading until later.

"The first hour of the morning is the rudder of the day."

**Henry Ward Beecher**
*1813-1887*
*Orator, writer*

- I have found that if I write a list of what I want to accomplish for the day, even for my discretionary time, I can accomplish more of the important tasks, leaving time to grow and to change. Once I set priorities, I find that I resist working off of somebody else's objectives.

- I've found that I need to take time to do it right the first time. As the old expression says, "There's never enough time to do it right, but there's always enough time to do it over."

"Take care in your minutes, and the hours will take care of themselves."

**Lord Chesterfield**
*1694-1773*
British statesman, author

- I must prevent *recurring crises*. If something "goes sideways" once a week, once a month, or once a year, the second or third time that happens, I realize that I have a recurring crisis on my hands and I must fix it.

## *Decide to beat procrastination and you will*

I encountered a classic example of procrastination when I interviewed a psychologist, who my client was considering hiring to head a department. As we were talking, it came up that he had been involved in a relationship with the same woman for twelve years.

Normally, a person's relationships aren't any of my business. In this case, I needed to explore further to see whether this managerial candidate was an indecisive person.

I learned his fiancée wanted to get married and that he loved her. When I asked why he hadn't married, he said, "I just had a little trouble deciding, making the commitment."

I asked him, "Why is it all right that as a clinician, you ask people to change, to make decisions, and to take on major changes in their life, and yet you have been putting off this decision for all of these years; what makes this all right?" He experienced a *moment of awareness*. I recommended that my client hire him and he got the job.

About three months later, I received a small card postmarked Maui, Hawaii that read, "We are pleased to announce our marriage in Maui, Hawaii." The psychologist had stopped procrastinating about his marriage.

When we decide to change, one of the real challenges is procrastination, putting off until tomorrow that which is often, but not always, distasteful. Procrastination has been referred to the "thief of time." It also prevents us from changing, growing and becoming.

When we procrastinate a task, we often begin to dread doing it even more as time passes.

I was working for the world's largest producer of day-old baby chicks for the egg industry. I was spending time in the field with some of their salespeople and in the office with their management team.

On this particular day, I was out in a remote area with Dave, their top salesperson, and we started talking about change, time and procrastination. He told me this story about when he first took over his territory:

His predecessor had sold 25,000 day-old baby chicks to an egg producer, and within two days, a number of the baby chicks were dead or dying. The farmer was absolutely beside himself, angry, upset and very worried that if it was an epidemic or a disease common to the poultry industry, it might spread to his flock.

Dave's predecessor did not return the egg producer's phone calls. The farmer called a competitor, who visited him and solved the problem. The egg producer then called Dave's firm, my client, and made it very clear that he was upset and would no longer do business with them.

Dave knew that he had to call on the farmer to at least apologize in person and make himself available for any solution that the farmer felt was necessary. He knew it was important to listen to this customer and experience his wrath in person.

Although his work called for him to be in the area near the farmer every six weeks, he kept driving past the angry customer's ranch, calling on other farmers. He never stopped to talk even though he knew he should. This went on for nine months.

Dave continually thought about that farmer, how angry he was, and what Dave's company had done to him. When he talked to a prospect or another customer his promises felt hollow to him. The unresolved situation affected his job and his home life. He would be out on his boat with his wife and children and start thinking about that customer relationship. One evening he and his wife had secured a babysitter and went out to dinner in a very special restaurant, complete with candles and wine. Dave couldn't get that farmer out of his mind.

*The things we avoid can begin to consume us*

Finally, he made a *decision.* He told me that in his car one day, he hit the steering wheel and said, "The next time I'm out there, I'm going to call on him." Six weeks later, Dave found himself driving up to the ranch, and he almost felt ill. As he was parking his car, the rancher came out. Dave introduced himself, and when it finally sunk in who he represented, the farmer took off on him, his predecessor, his company and his products. He sprinkled his words liberally with profanity.

I asked Dave how it felt. He said the longer the farmer spoke, the harsher he became. But the abuse was liberating. Dave said it was like standing under a warm shower. It was so cleansing, so beautiful that it was almost spiritual.

I asked him the obvious, "Why, because you faced him?"

He said, *"No, because I faced myself."*

## When we become aware that we are procrastinating, it's important for us to face ourselves – if we expect to grow.

"If we open a quarrel between the past and the present, we shall find we have lost the future."

**Winston Churchill**
*1874-1965*
*British statesman*

Dave's story illustrates is the importance of making a decision to beat procrastination. Until we make that decision, the situation can go on and on.

It can be hard to make decisions, and time-consuming. Here are a few techniques I've found that help:

- If possible make decisions in your *prime time*: the hours when you are in top form, have the clearest perspective, and think faster and better.

- Don't invest more time and energy in a decision than it's worth. Realize that it doesn't have to be perfect; most of us are paid to get results, not to be perfect. Make decisions even when some of the facts are missing. In life, some risk is inevitable.

- Stop dealing with the past, rehashing former decisions, explaining bad ones, salvaging poor investments that ought to be written off and forgotten. Use the past as a guide to the future, not as an excuse for not dealing with it.

Recognize that *indecision is often a form of procrastination*. There is a time for deliberation and a time for action. When it's time to act, act with boldness and move on. Sometimes we make mistakes. That's a fact of life.

## If we're not making mistakes, we're not doing anything significant.

### The tyranny of the urgent

C. Northcote Parkinson became famous for his law, "Work expands to fill the time allotted." If we don't exercise control, the easy-to-do and convenient activities will take most of our time.

If we're going to make time for life-changing growth, it becomes necessary to leverage our time and use it productively. Unfortunately, we often get caught in the *Tyranny of the urgent*. Urgent items are those that appear to have a time limit and have to be done immediately. The problem is, they are not important. A teenager, for example, has homework. This is important and should have priority. But his favorite video is on sale at the mall (a one-hour round trip) and the sale ends tonight. He will opt for getting the video (urgent but not important) and delay the homework (important).

The chart below will help you characterize which activities are important to your success and which are urgent but not important:

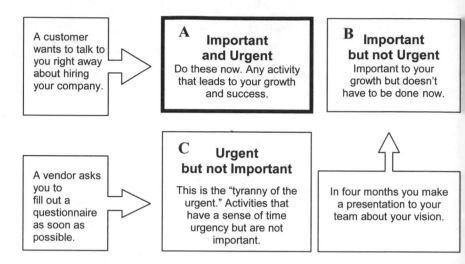

## *Summary*

When we establish an image in our mind, we conform to the expectations of that image because we have a need to be consistent, even if it is to consistently fail.

It becomes just as hard to break a pattern of success as it does a pattern of failure.

If you feed your subconscious success, that's what you are going to get.

I found my payday when I realized the key was the pictures I held in my mind.

You can have anything you want; you just can't have everything.

If I'm not making mistakes, I'm not doing anything significant.

When we become aware that we are procrastinating, it's important for us to face ourselves – if we expect to grow.

# Stage Six: Decision

If you are reading this section and are on the verge of making an important decision about a change in your life, congratulations! It has taken a lot of work to get to this point. We've had to:

- Recognize through our **discomfort** a need to change
- **Analyze** our situation, overcoming our urge to be right and blame others
- **Explore** the consequences of change by setting new goals
- **Experiment** with changing our self-image, which probably required us to leave our comfort zone and make sacrifices, as well as make time to experiment and change

This is the stage where the rubber meets the road. Our change has gained tremendous momentum and the only thing holding us back from making the decision is fear.

## *Decide to face what you fear and you will change*

To reach our full potential, we must find a way through our fear. At some point in time, we must plant our feet and confront it. Once we do, fear often fades.

Here's my story: heights used to terrify me.

As a young man, I had an opportunity to spend a week working with a steeplejack in a sawmill. A steeplejack is someone who builds, repairs and performs maintenance jobs at heights. We worked welding reinforcements on a crane that traveled on railroad tracks through the yard in the sawmill. It was forty-five feet in the air, but the first night that I climbed to the top of the crane, it seemed like a thousand.

As I brought the steeplejack welding rods and other tools, I attached them to a pack on my back and held on for dear life as I inched across the two-by-eight planks to where he was working.

I was terrified of falling. Climbing up the ladder on the edge of the crane was not that much of an ordeal; but when I swung in to scamper across the boards, I *visualized* falling to the tracks below.

In the first five minutes on this job, I learned something I had long suspected: that I had a fear of heights. The first time the steeplejack directed me to bring him some welding rods, and I started to make my way across the planks, I was almost paralyzed.

I could have walked off the job and avoided the fear, but the steeplejack was paying me $1.50 an hour. In those days, that was good pay.

The first couple of days on the job were dreadful. Then, something wondrous happened on the third.

*To beat your fears, you must make a decision to face them*

As I was edging across the two by eights to bring the steeplejack a tool, I actually let go. Instead of inching across on my hands and knees, I *made the decision* to walk in a crouched position. The distance from the stringers to the bottom of the deck was about five feet and I was over six feet tall, so in order to move, I had to crouch or walk hunched over.

I *decided* to face my fears and, each time I did, the sheer terror began to fade.

I could have talked about, written about, discussed, or even sought counseling for my fear of heights. But the only way I knew how to keep my job as a helper for the steeplejack was by *doing* it.[§]

On the third day, as I crouched and brought him the welding rods and special tools that he needed, I was aware that I had overcome my fear. By the second half of that shift, he asked me if I wanted to try my hand at welding. I had never welded anything and did not see myself as a mechanic, but I said "yes." On the fourth day, I was scrambling on the two-by-eights comfortably and felt at ease. On the fifth, I actually looked forward to going to work and moved freely forty-five feet in the air.

I faced the fear and beat it.

The job taught me a great deal about myself. Later in my life, when I had to make a presentation, cold-call a prospect, visit with the IRS, or whatever, I used what I had learned working with the steeplejack to face my fear.

**When we talk about change, we are talking about growing and, to grow, we have to overcome our fears.**

### *We must renew the decision to confront our fears on a regular basis*

Overcoming my fear of heights was a significant personal victory. However, I learned that I had to repeat that experience to maintain the same level of courage. Like so many growth experiences, it's not a case of accomplishing it once and enjoying a lifetime of benefits. Confronting our fears is a decision we must "renew" on a regular basis.

---

[§] By now, OSHA would have shut that job down because it simply wasn't safe. At the very least, I would have probably been secured with a harness and safety line.

**If we don't continue to face that which causes us angst, discomfort, or stress, chances are, it will return.**

Around the time of my fiftieth birthday, I found myself once again uncomfortable with the thought of being off the ground. So I decided to take on some challenges to work past it.

The first was to parachute out of an aircraft.

On a Sunday morning, I went to the airfield where I had made reservations for ground school, the flight and the jump. I was nervous. Thought of parachuting was very disconcerting.

The preparation for a parachute jump has great parallels with getting ready for any other big undertaking in life. First, we had to train and *visualize* Bill, the jumpmaster, had us climb up a tower, close our eyes and jump into pea gravel. Jumping off that platform, first at six and then at eight feet in the air, was a challenge for me. But it was certainly great training. If he had taken me up in the plane first, without the preparation, it might have been more than I could handle. But after practicing on the small platform, closing my eyes and jumping, I was ready. Or at least I thought I was.

As I was walking around the ready room, the place you go before proceeding to the airplane, I was trying to act nonchalant. But when I caught my reflection in a window, I saw that I was as pale as an old, bleached-out flour sack.

At that point, a mentor appeared.

Another jumper in our group, Rob Lee, looked at me and asked, "First jump, eh?"

I said, "Yes, and I'm experiencing a lot of emotion about all of this."

*Train and prepare for your personal victories*

He said, "You're going to love it. It will be the most exciting, the most exotic – bordering on erotic – experience you've ever had. I've jumped a lot of times, but I haven't jumped for thirty days, and I have to prove myself again. That's why I'm here. You have to stay certified; otherwise you have to go back through the class just like it's your first time."

He went on to describe the experience of jumping: "When you reach forward and grab that wing strut with your two feet on that step, it's the most exhilarating, feeling you've ever had. With the roar of that engine about three feet from your head and the wind going under your helmet, the prop wash blowing you, you are going to have the most wonderful feeling.

"When the jumpmaster reaches down and taps you, and you simply fall backwards, and when that static line pulls your chute open, then you look up and see the parachute above you, it is a moment of victory.

"As you float down, you can't hear a sound. Then, as you pull the shrouds and direct yourself to your landing area, you have the power of knowing that you are steering, you are in control of your own future, your own destiny."

I said, "Rob, if it's okay to ask, what do you do for a living?"

He matter-of-factly replied, "I own a company called the Independent Blasting Service. I blow up anything I can get my hands on. Did you see that big building that they just blew up downtown last weekend?"

I told him that I had been looking at the building when I heard the explosion. Then, it just disappeared from view among the buildings surrounding it and I couldn't see it any longer.

Rob said, "That's what I do. I'll blow up anything."

I asked him, because I could see he had a wonderful sense of humor, "When you and your team are blowing things up, on the average, how often do you make a mistake?"

And he dryly answered, "Ralph, on the average, just once."

Rob, with his enthusiasm, humor, and reassurance, helped ease my fears. And he was right about the jump.

When I got into that small aircraft, I thought of a crop duster I had seen around forty years before. This one seemed as old. It didn't have a door, and three jumpers and the jumpmaster were packed into this small aircraft behind the pilot. We sat on the floor, and I leaned up against a bulkhead until it was my turn to jump.

I've found that when I'm going to face something difficult, that it's all right for me to draw on humor to help me through it.

About five minutes before the jump, I hollered over the engine roar coming in from the open doorway, "Hey, Bill, I gave you a check when I arrived this morning. If it's returned for whatever reason don't worry about it. Just run it through again; it was just a computer error or something."

Bill hollered back, "Hey, Ralph, same thing with that parachute. If it doesn't open, for whatever reason, don't worry about it, just bring it back and we'll repack it for free, and we'll run you through again at no charge."

*Humor helps*

Parachuting is like raising kids; you've got to get it right the first time.

I made the jump successfully and will never forget, in Rob's words, the "exhilarating experience."

To celebrate my fiftieth birthday, I wanted to climb one of the highest mountains in the Northwest. It was another way to face my fear of heights. I chose Mt. Rainier, over 14,000 feet in elevation. This would be new, different, challenging, and somewhat dangerous. It was an opportunity to change and grow.

Like the parachute jump, the climb required training and preparation: I learned how to use an ice axe to stop sliding down the mountain if I fell; I got used to working at higher altitudes in order to stave off altitude sickness; I trained to be comfortable when roped to other people. (Early on, I found out why they rope us together: It's to stop the smart ones from going home!)

Going up that magnificent mountain, I faced a lot of fears: the fear of avalanche, exhaustion, and extreme height. I made it to the top on the first ascent, which says a lot about the skill of those leading the climb.

These experiences held three important lessons about how to face fear:

1.  Get the right person to guide you through the process (my parachute trainer, the mountain team leaders) and, most importantly, strive to see the task from their perspective.

2.  Preparation is vital, because it builds safety into your quest and keeps you organized

3.  The fear subsides when you face it, but at some point, you may have to decide to repeat the experience to maintain your courage

### *From novice fisherman to charter boat captain: The anatomy of a journey*

A salmon journeys upstream to spawn, fighting currents and never giving up. Facing fear is a journey. Before we are done, we often find ourselves in a place we never believed we could be.

On one such journey, I started out as an amateur salmon fisher and wound up a charter boat captain, with our son Jon as first mate. Along the way, I learned about facing fear and change.

This journey started when Bob Nakao, a sales manager at my old firm, invited me to go salmon fishing with him. With my Norwegian heritage – my mother grew up on a farm in Norway near a fjord and helped my grandfather catch codfish – I'd always been drawn towards the sea and fishing.

Still, I had been salmon fishing just a few times and had caught only very small salmon, usually too small to keep. Bob regaled me with stories about how good the salmon fishing was where we would go and how we probably would catch some large silvers or kings. Bob had grown up on the water. He had run pleasure boats, worked as a charter boat captain, and had fished in Alaska.

We drove Bob's 19-foot boat on a trailer from Seattle to Ilwaco, a quaint fishing village located on the southwest corner of Washington State. After we put the boat in the water, we headed down the Columbia River and into the sea.

We soon noticed a small amount of water in the bottom of the boat, but not enough to attract much attentin. It's not unusual for a little rainwater to gather on the deck of a boat.

Bob throttled it back and we began to drift. Between the tidal action and the wind, you could get enough action on your line to keep the bait moving. After about half an hour of popping the motor in and out of gear, which is called "mooching and drifting," we were catching salmon at a healthy rate. We'd already put four in the boat out of our limit of six when we noticed that what had been a little bit of water at the bottom of the boat now covered the deck.

The water alarmed Bob, who finally understood that we were sinking. Our pleasant fishing trip now had an edge to it: fear. There were no other boats in sight.

We were taking on water through the transom, the back section of the boat. That particular design of boat has two drain plugs that screw in through the stern at the waterline. The plugs are taken out if the boat fills with rain so that the water can flow out through the back end when it is hauled on a trailer. That is also the principle behind "self bailing." To self bail, you need to get the boat moving at a good speed so that it will plane, making the water in the boat flow back and out through the drain holes.

*When mooching and drifting, make sure there isn't a hole In the bottom of your boat*

Bob realized that whoever had used the boat last had taken the drain plugs out. He started the engine and had me steer across the pounding waves at 25 to 30 mph. while he searched for the plugs. The water ran out through the stern as we shot across the waves and the boat was almost fully drained by the time Bob found and inserted the plugs.

That experience was the greatest single lesson that I had for owning and operating a commercial boat. Because of it, I developed a *safety check-off list* for operating small boats.

*Use a check-off list when embracing change*

I have flown in Lockheed P2-Vs in a patrol squadron. Many times, I observed the pilots make a visual check-off, physically touching certain parts of the plane to make sure that it was safe to fly. They used a list called a "plane captain's check-off list." The idea was to test everything possible while it was still on the ground.

**When you embrace change and enter a new adventure, prepare a check-off list. This**

**list will build safety into your quest and, also important, keep you organized.**

Overall, I had a great time with Bob, and began to rent boats on weekends to go salmon fishing with our son Jon, who was then eight years old.

After gaining some experience, we moved our fishing from Ilwaco to Westport, which advertised itself as the salmon capital of the world. We began to go out in charter boats.

Charter boats range in size from thirty to sixty feet, and can hold up to thirty passengers. It's a great way to fish for salmon – exciting and much safer than going out in a small fishing boat. Charter boats are enclosed and have a toilet and other amenities. They are much more comfortable than small craft.

As Jon and I went on our charter boat trips, we noticed that many of the charter boat captains had a tendency to develop a rude attitude. They were curt with their customers, had short tempers and were easily irked.

There didn't seem to be any relationship between their seamanship skills, their fishing abilities, and the way they treated their guests. Sometimes the best seamen, in terms of navigating the vessel and catching salmon, were the rudest and most ill tempered

One Saturday, Jon (now ten years old) and I went fishing on a charter boat. We were the only guests on a boat that would normally hold six.

Usually each guest has one pole and the captain fishes with a "boat pole." The boat pole was hot that day, having landed a few salmon. The captain told Jon that if he hadn't caught a salmon, the next fish on the boat pole would be his.

Soon after that there was a strike on the boat pole. The captain handed the pole to Jon, who started to play it.

After about ten minutes, Jon had the fish close enough to the boat to see it. It was a huge salmon. We could see it was hooked on the top of its back just behind the dorsal fin, indicating that the fish had slapped at the bait in order to stun it and had somehow got the hook lodged in its back.

With the hook in that position, the fish was free to swim and fight anyway it wanted, which it is unable to do when hooked in the mouth. Getting it on the boat was going to take some effort. The captain took the pole from Jon and began to play the salmon. I was so aware of how I felt: disappointed. I wasn't angry, but what was transpiring was not what was promised.

*A winner is a person who does what they say they are going to do*

The captain asked me to go to the bridge and steer the vessel. I did, and for the next hour and a half, the captain played the salmon.

The salmon fought hard, diving towards the bottom of the ocean and then running away from the boat. The captain played it well. I kept the boat headed in the same direction as the fish, allowing the captain to keep tension on the line. We finally netted the largest salmon I had ever seen. It was 54 pounds, 12 ounces.

The captain ended up keeping it. And we ended up never using his boat again.

Those charter boat captains taught me a lot of lessons. I learned that you could be the best seaman in the world, but if you are rude to your customers, they will not return. More importantly, I learned no matter how painful or how difficult the decision, keep your word.

For years after that, when we would visit Westport, we would stop by the office of the charter firm where the salmon was mounted and displayed on the wall; it was one of the largest salmon ever caught in the area.

*As you confront fear, be aware of others around you*

The lesson Jon and I both learned was much more valuable than the trophy could ever be worth. When we're initiating change, we want to be aware of our attitude, how we're reacting mentally and how we treat other people when they're stressed because of change.

## When we promise something and it's under our control, we keep our word.

After chartering boats for awhile, we finally bought our own – a twenty-two foot long Chris-Craft with a high-powered in-board engine – the next step in our journey.

Eventually, we went from amateur status to professional. It started one day on the way back from a fishing trip. We noticed a sign hanging in the window of a charter office: CHARTER CAPTAIN WANTED. Jon and I went inside and learned that a trucking company owned a charter boat and was looking for a captain to run it on heavy charter days.

I realized I could do that job, so I set about getting a charter boat captain's license. I had to prove I had a certain amount of experience on the water, and I had to pass a test administered by the Coast Guard. I failed the test three times. Before I took the test a fourth time, I found a course to help me prepare. I received a near-perfect score.

*When I am going to change, I have to be willing to fail*

When we are going to change and grow, we have to be willing to fail. I learned never to give up. Because I kept failing the test, I finally found a course to help me prepare professionally. It was a proud moment when I received my license to become a charter boat captain.

I had seen the "captain wanted" sign in the fall and was licensed four months later, in the springtime. I began to pilot the trucking company's boat on holidays, weekends and vacations with Jon as my first mate.

Working as first mate on a charter boat was great training for Jon. We put into practice what we had learned from our experiences fishing with previous captains and crews: the value of focusing on the other person and the importance of staying with a goal, even after you have failed before.

As Jon baited hooks and helped the guests on the vessel, he learned to work with people who were seasick, who were brusque, who were in a bad mood because they had not caught any fish. He worked with both old people and young children.

Jon's journey took him into sales and management. His dealings with people who were sick, moody or euphoric from catching a big fish were a great study for his future career.

All the lessons we had learned came to fruition one dramatic Saturday afternoon. About an hour before we were to go into port, a ferocious rain started to fall and the wind began to blow. The Coast Guard radioed that they wanted everyone off the ocean.

Heading back toward the mouth of the river, the bar looked extremely rough. Halfway over the bar, I noticed a boat ahead of us about twice our size. As it rode up to the top of a twenty-foot wave, I saw the wave break in front of it. The water fell away from the bottom of the vessel. For a moment, I watched the props spin and then saw the boat slam down into the trough before starting up the crest of another wave.

I knew at that moment, that within a minute or two, I would be in exactly the same position. There was no question of turning back. Going forward was the only way to get out of this crisis. I knew that I needed to maintain speed at the top of the wave and hold the wheel steady so that it was not jerked when the boat crashed down.

*Sometimes there is no choice but to go forward*

I still recall what it was like to be twenty feet in the air, knowing that the boat would soon slam down on the water below.

In that frightening instant, I could see my journey, from fishing with a buddy in a leaky boat to becoming a professional charter boat captain. It was clear that at each stage, I had made a **decision** to face my fears and advance. I had learned much along the way:

129

- How to work with all types of people in a positive manner
- How to empathize and see things through other people's eyes
- If you don't panic, and if you stand up to your fears, there is almost always a way back to a safe harbor

Our Christ-Craft crashed down, hitting the water with great force, but stayed together. I held the wheel steady and soon we were at the harbor.

## *Summary*

When we talk about change, we are talking about growing and, to grow, we have to overcome our fears.

If I don't continue to face that which causes me fear, discomfort, or stress, chances are, it will return.

When you embrace change and enter a new adventure, prepare a check-off list. This list will build safety into your quest and, also important, keep you organized.

When we promise something and it's under our control, we keep our word.

If you don't panic, and if you stand up to your fears, there is almost always a way back to a safe harbor

# Stage Seven: Commitment

This stage is about maintaining the gains we have already achieved. When we make a change, we sometimes push back against it and try to figure out ways to revert back to the way we were. This resistance is often subconscious. If we are able to persist, then the change takes root in our lives and blossoms. This is the stage at which we can either make excuses — what I call "getting our story straight" — or "close the loop" and make the change.

### *Find the reason(s) why you should keep going, and you will keep going*

Sitting in a Broadway theater waiting for the show *Miss Saigon* to begin, I started a conversation with the man seated next to me, an architect who practices in Manhattan. He asked me why I was in New York. I told him that I was going to run the New York City marathon the next morning.

Almost imperceptibly, his eyes went to the gray in my hair. I was in my sixties. While I waited for the show to start, I felt the slight nag of a persistent sciatic nerve in my left hip. I wondered whether what I was about to do was advisable.

After the show, I returned to my room at the New York Athletic Club, which is in the middle of Manhattan, across the street from Central Park, and about a half mile from the finish line of the marathon. As I lay in bed that night, before the marathon, I thought about how my life had changed in the last forty years.

The next morning I was up at 5:00 a.m. I caught the bus from Manhattan to the staging area on Staten Island. It takes 45 minutes to get from Manhattan to Staten Island by bus, crossing the Veranzano Bridge on the way. I had a four-hour wait in the staging area until the race began. Cold wind and rain pelted down. As I sat on the chilly grass near the starting line, I felt the rain seep through my clothes. Ay sixty-four, I had only one concern: Can I finish? It had been many years since I had attempted an organized run of any kind, much less a marathon.

Then, I realized that I could still deal with uncertainty and found beauty in the moment. I became filled with gratitude to be alive.

I thought about how thankful I was to be able to even attempt to run a marathon at my age. I realized that I was fortunate to still have my health and the opportunity to fly to New York City and attempt the race, when so many others do not. I knew that running a marathon is something that relatively few people have a chance to do.

At 10:50 a.m., the starting gun sounded. We ran through five boroughs starting on Staten Island, through Brooklyn, Queens, Manhattan, the Bronx, and back into Manhattan.

After about twelve miles, I felt like quitting. "I don't need this," I thought. "I'm too old to be out here. What am I trying to prove?" At some point in any marathon many of us wonder: "Maybe this would be a good time to pack it in. This might be a good time to walk into an aid station and catch a ride back."

What kept me going was a thought in my mind. I wondered what I would tell my granddaughters and grandsons if I quit. Would I tell them, "Your grandfather is a quitter?" Perhaps something could be made up that would sell. Before I began making a story about not finishing, I realized how important it was to close the loop and finish the race.

At that point, I found the reason why I had to keep on going, and I made the *commitment* that I was going to finish the race.

Between eighteen and twenty miles, I started getting it back. When I entered Central Park, after about twenty-three miles, I thought it was as great an event as I had ever participated in.

I've found that the feeling of pushing past my resistance and overcoming myself is just about as good as it gets.

In all, 27,480 people finished that race. I was the 25,906[th] to cross the finish line. Out of 545 people in my age bracket, (sixty to seventy), I was the 443rd person to finish. The winner of the marathon that year was probably back home in Kenya sipping tea by the time I finished. No matter. I had kept my promise to myself.

After we have made a decision to change, we pass through a **Commitment** stage. After all the work it took to get through **Hypothermia**, **Discomfort**, **Analysis**, **Exploring**, **Experimenting** and **Decision**, we want to marshal our resources and commit to going all the way.

### *Getting your story straight*

Sometimes we need a good story — a story that sells. Forty years before I ran that marathon, I spent time in a jail cell, learning how to get my story straight.

The jail cell was the US Marine Corps brig in the island of Guam, in the South Pacific. I had been court-martialed and sentenced to hard labor. As I lay on the hard bunk, I thought about how I ended up there.

I remembered the words of Lieutenant West, the convening officer of my court martial. After I had pled guilty, the testimony had been heard, and the sentence delivered, he said: "Guam hasn't been very good to you, has it son? It's not a great place for a young single man with a lot of time on his hands and inclination toward alcohol abuse." With these words, he handed me my story, airtight and unshakable. I had failed because Guam was not a good place for a young man.

Lying in that cell, I was glad that my fiancée and family back in the states couldn't see me. But if they could, I would have told them: It was Guam. It was the boredom and frustration of living on the island. After twenty months, what would you expect? *I was getting my story straight.*

I could even have told them that it wasn't really my fault, that it was Frank's. Frank was the man who slept in the bunk next to mine on the base. He worked for the supply division, in a cold storage plant that warehoused food for the commissary, mess hall, and the ships in Agana Harbor. Frank was about 21 years old and a big man, at six-foot seven and 260 pounds. When you live less than two feet away from another person for a number of months, you come to think you know them pretty well, and we soon became great friends.

"Do not weep; do not wax indignant. Understand."

**Baruch Spinoza,** philosopher

Frank was an ideal companion. Despite a tendency to become a little belligerent when he drank too much, he was generally soft-spoken and a decent shipmate.

I didn't know it at first, but he was also a thief. It always seemed like Frank had extra cash, but it never occurred to me how he might be getting it. For months, he and two high-ranking petty officers stole cases of ham, turkey and steak from the warehouse and sold them to local restaurants up in Agana.

They had a great scheme going and might never have been caught, except that they got greedy. One night, they loaded a Navy panel truck full of stolen ham, turkey, and steaks, and tried to leave the base. Frank had full clearance to drive Navy vehicles, but they had overloaded the truck so much that it was almost riding on its axles; the suspension was not designed to carry such a heavy load. They were stopped and searched on their way off the base. When the guard opened the back of the truck, he found the stolen Navy meat.

Frank was placed under arrest, court-martialed, and sentenced to eight years in a naval prison. While he awaited transfer back to the U.S., he was locked up in the same brig that I would later occupy.

On the Thursday that would turn out to be a very fateful day in my life, I returned to the barracks around 4:15 p.m. I had a normal routine that I followed. I worked as a manager in the supply depot during the day and as base movie operator at night.

There was a free outdoor movie every night at 7:30 p.m. My daily job was to pick up the movie, show it on time, and then return it to the movie exchange. The movie operator's job was one of the best jobs on the base. I didn't have to stand any night watches and I earned an extra $100 a month, almost equal to my base salary.

The Korean War was just winding down, and the Navy wanted servicemen to "ship over" and re-enlist. I knew I didn't want to extend my time in the Navy. I longed for the day when my eighteen months on Guam would end, and I would transfer back to the States for the last six months of my four-year enlistment, which is what I had been promised. I had learned a few weeks earlier that my transfer to the States was cancelled, and I was to spend my last six months in the Navy in Guam.

I was extremely upset. My frustration was so great that when I learned of an opportunity to extend my time in the Navy for another year, and then get rotated back to the United States at the end of my eighteen-month tour, I immediately signed up. A number of other men who ranked the same as me signed up on the same day.

When I arrived back at the barracks that Thursday, the Duty Master at Arms greeted and congratulated me. Out of all the people who had signed up to extend, I was the only one who received orders so far. He told me that the next day I was to check out, go to the Navy airfield in Agana, and fly to Hawaii. From there, I would fly back to the States, receive thirty days leave, and then report to the Naval Aviation Missile Test Center in Point Mugu, California.

I had mixed feelings. I was ecstatic at the thought of getting off the island, flying home, marrying my fiancée, and leading a somewhat more normal life. But I also realized that I would have to serve an extra year in the Navy, which left me feeling less than enthusiastic. Before I went to run the movie that night, I packed my sea bag.

"Give not over thy mind to heaviness, and afflict not thyself in thine own counsel."

Ecclesiasticus 30:21

About five minutes before the movie ended, I received a phone call from my friend Frank. He had been transferred from the brig to the sick bay for psychiatric observation because of depression. He wanted me to meet him outside, by the corner of the dispensary and take him down to a village to have a few drinks. I told him how elated I was to be going home, and he seemed genuinely happy for me. I packed up the movie, put it in the backseat of my car, and headed for the dispensary.

"The farther behind I leave the past, the closer I am to forging my own character."

Isabelle Eberhardt

Frank was waiting for me in the shadows near the corner of the building. We went out the gate and drove up to a village to drink for about three hours. On the way back, we stopped at a drive-in to have a hamburger. After that, I planned to drop Frank off back at the dispensary and get some sleep in the barracks before reporting to the Naval air station to fly out the next day.

Soon after the waitress placed our food on my window, I noticed a number of Marine Corps vehicles had pulled into the parking lot of the drive-in. "I think we have a problem," I told Frank. I assumed the Marines and Armed Services Police were checking ID and liberty cards. All non-married, enlisted personnel had to be off the streets and back in the barracks by 11:00 p.m. It was now close to 1:00 a.m. When the Marine came to our car, I told him, "I'm the base movie operator, we just secured the movie booth and we're having a hamburger before we turn in for the night."

What we didn't know was that there were half-hour bunk checks on Frank in sickbay. The Armed Services Police, the Shore Patrol, the Guam police and the United States Marshall were all looking for Frank.

The Marine pulled his .45 out of the holster, slammed a shell into the chamber, which automatically cocked it, and pointed it at us. As he held the gun in his right hand, he took the tray off the window very slowly with his left hand and set it on the ground. He then ordered us out of the car and told us to "assume the position."

The Marines were very upset as they took us to headquarters for processing. The Navy views aiding and abetting the escape of a general court martial prisoner as a very serious offense. When I tried to explain that we were not escaping, but only taking a little unauthorized leave, there was little understanding or sympathy.

I woke up the next morning in a cell next to Frank. Within a day, my division officer had me released from the brig, while my best friend got my shore duty in California. I lost my job as movie operator and was restricted to the barracks.

I stayed on restriction for sixty days awaiting my preliminary hearing. My division officer told me that he had spoken on my behalf, and many of the charges were going to be dropped. Instead of a court martial, I was to receive some additional restriction and then be allowed to "coast out" the rest of my time in the Navy.

On the day I was scheduled to attend my hearing, I asked my division chief petty officer if I could leave work early that day to get some rest. I told him that I had wanted to shower and put on clean whites for my 1:00

p.m. hearing. He could see that I had been drinking the night before and was in bad shape.

The chief let me go. But instead of returning to the barracks, I went to a little village with a couple of friends and drank straight whiskey. At about 11:00 a.m., I headed back to the barracks to clean up and get some rest. When I got to the gate, I'm certain to this day that the Marine flagged me through when he saw the sticker on my windshield.

He later testified that he had not. There was an Armed Services Police detachment vehicle right behind me, they gave me the siren and lights and pulled me over. Instead of returning to the barracks to prepare for my hearing, I was brought to the dispensary, where the doctor determined that I was intoxicated. I went back to the brig and finally back to my division. When I finally got to see the captain, he was irate. In two minutes, I was court-martialed.

I was fined and sentenced to hard labor. Life in a Marine brig, especially for someone who has aided and abetted an escape, was not pleasant. The Marines were embarrassed by the escape and very angry with me.

At one point, they assigned me to a special punishment detail. I was to remove the paint from an asphalt driveway by using a forty-four pound building block, which they called a "holy stone," and a little solvent they gave me to remove the paint. I scraped the asphalt between two Quonset huts with circular motions, laboring in the scorching midday sun.

The Marine brig aims to retrain prisoners. From 5:00 a.m. until lights out at 9:30 p.m., there was a Marine in my face most of the time. Part of the process involves humiliation and breaking down the ego.

The brig did not have its own kitchen. We were transported three times a day, under heavy guard, to a special section in the common base mess hall. We walked in lock step, keeping a cadence with other prisoners, right hands resting on the prisoner's shoulder preceding us. We ate without talking, our left wrist always held on the edge of the table.

You might think that my time in the brig was a learning experience for me. It wasn't. The day I got out, I went to Agana, drank excessively and narrowly escaped going right back in.

Being marched in lock step by Marines carrying loaded shotguns and side arms should have taught me something. It really had no effect. There was no opening in my mind to consider that perhaps that I could be wrong, or that I could change. I had my story straight: *Guam had not been very good to me.*

As long as it was someone else's fault, then the brig, the hard labor, the humiliation – it was all OK. I told myself that I had simply been helping Frank, a good friend. I blamed Guam, the Navy, being away from home, everything but myself. Nothing was my fault.

> "We can actually put the essence of neurosis in a single word: blaming – or damning."
>
> **Albert Ellis & Robert A. Harper**, *A Guide to Rational Living*

### Keeping your story straight blocks you to the possibility of positive change and growth.

Some years later, I realized I had my "Made-a-Million, Lost-a-Million Story" straight. This time, I was able to see how getting my story straight wasn't necessarily getting me closer to my goals.

It came after my 84-year-old mother suffered a fall that limited her independence. In order for my mother to continue living at home, I hired a caregiver for her, a Norwegian immigrant named Carla. Carla wanted to work as a live-in nurse, while she considered applying for citizenship.

One day, as I was visiting my mother, I began speaking with Carla. When she asked me what I did for a living, I told her I worked as a management, marketing and sales consultant.

When she asked how long I had been a consultant and what I did prior to this, I related my version of the story I had rehearsed in my head.

I told her that I had worked for a large company with hundreds of employees in branches covering twenty-three states and Canada. I told her about how my partner had been hit by a boat in the water, had lost his leg and that in the ensuing weeks, the board brought in a new chairman, fired my partner, and ultimately, the company failed. New owners took over.

"Take your life in your own hands, and what happens? A terrible thing: no one to blame."

**Erica Jong,**
*author*

I told her that even though the company had failed, I was offered the position of CEO with the new company that had formed out of the old one. I had chosen to move on and start my consulting practice.

After she heard my story, Carla said, "But it wasn't your fault."

*That was precisely the point I wanted to convey.* I realized at that moment that I had my story straight. I'd made it clear that it wasn't my fault. I had tailored the story to imply that I was the victim of circumstance and fate.

What I knew then and know now is that it was much more complicated than that. Yes, management had failed, but I was a significant part of the management team. I had shaded the version so that I came out smelling like roses. I was deceiving Carla, and I was deceiving myself.

We can spend a lifetime getting our story straight

After a lifetime of practice, I had learned to get my story straight, to rationalize my failure. It enabled me to explain away anything that had not worked out my way.

But unlike my experience in the Guam brig, I decided then that I no longer wanted to play the blame

140

game. I realized I could stop my great need to make excuses.

I decided to accept accountability for what happens in my life. I decided to change what I can and accept and live with the rest. You never become a "loser" until you blame someone else for your failure. When you start that, there is no end to the blame.

**Our commitment to changing begins with accepting responsibility for whatever happens in our lives.**

### Closing the loop

To really make a **commitment**, we need to go from getting our stories straight to *closing the loop*.

I was consulting for a company with a sales force of about 100 people. The top salesperson was in a tailspin. Named "salesperson of the year," for the previous two years, he had the lowest sales in the company and was barely hanging on to his job. No one could figure out why he had fallen so far, so fast.

Finally the president of the company, a man whom I had worked with for fifteen years, called him into his office. He asked his once star salesperson, "Why has a person with your history of ability and success gone from being a top sales performer to almost last in the company?"

Without hesitating, the salesperson told him, "It's you. I don't like working for you, I don't like you, I don't like what this company has become, and I was trying to hurt you. I wanted to see you fail. I knew that if I stopped being effective, it would cut into production, it would impact your numbers and performance, and would cause problems for you. "

The president was hurt. He had no idea that any of his hundreds of employees disliked him so much. Trying to conceal his emotion, he asked the salesperson, "What are you going to do now?"

Once again, without looking away, blinking, or hesitating, the salesperson replied, "I'm going to change. Once again, I am going to be number one. I'm going to get back on top of the ladder and stay there."

"What made you change your mind?" the president asked.

"You're just not worth it," the salesperson replied. "You're just not worth ruining my life, my career, and my health. I'm going back to work and I'm going to forget about this and once again become number one." And he did! He became the top salesman and enjoyed tremendous personal success.

By doing what was necessary to be successful, even to the point of discarding his anger, he **closed the loop** for himself. This is a powerful concept. The salesperson could have been defined by his rapid decline, or his anger with the President of the company. Instead, his choice to regain his top sales position by closing the loop is what defined him.

In his book, *Emotional Intelligence*, Daniel Goleman, tells of a test given to 4-year-olds. Researchers placed the children in a room and watched them through a one-way mirror. A researcher gave each child a marshmallow and left them alone. The children were told that the ones who did not eat their marshmallows while the researcher was gone would get a second one when he returned.

Some of the children ate their marshmallows immediately, before the researcher was even out the door. Others did not. They looked away, placed their marshmallows to the side, fiddled, played games and resisted the temptation to eat them. They were willing to postpone pleasure, or to "close the loop," to do what was necessary to achieve a subsequent reward.

Fifteen years later, when the members of the group were of college age, they were again contacted and interviewed. The results were astounding.

Those who had not eaten the marshmallows were the leaders, the best students, the best conversationalists, the most outgoing, and the most successful in all areas of their lives.

Those who had eaten the marshmallow, as a group, were more withdrawn, less socially adjusted, and had scored an average of 200 points lower on the Scholastic Aptitude Test than those who had not.

The study indicated that the emotional predisposition of children has as much to do with their future success as their intelligence. These were children who knew, from an early age, how to "close the loop."

One of the most truly gifted young men that I have ever worked with taught me a lot about the importance of closing the loop.

I worked with this young man, a friend, for many years and got to know him very well. He was bright, handsome, articulate, an accomplished athlete and a decorated war hero. When I first crossed paths with him, he lived in a beautiful home inside a gated country club community. He had become very wealthy.

As we worked together, we discussed our earlier years. In high school, he had been All-State in football, baseball and basketball. He had been offered scholarships to many major universities because of his athletic ability. But he stopped playing football in his junior year in high school. He said he quit because he had a lousy coach.

We talked about the influence of his family, in particular his father. While he loved and cared for his father, his father had not been a success in the areas that are usually used as a benchmark – job, career, community service, church, home life, marital relations. His family could best be described as "dysfunctional."

Rather than accepting any of the scholarships offered to him, he chose to work at a gas station after high school. From there he was drafted. He went to war and earned many medals, including the Silver Star. He told me that the war had left such a bitter taste in his mouth that, one evening, after long reflection, he burned his medals.

"When a man points a finger at someone else, he should remember that four of his fingers are pointing at himself."

**Louis Nizer**

The all-too-familiar pattern of blaming someone else had started for him. It was his family, the coach, the war, the government, but never his responsibility. I say this because I myself have been a blamer. From being a prisoner in Guam to being a "former" millionaire, it was always somebody else's doing, and certainly not mine.

When my young friend returned from the war, he went back to work at the gas station, where he was soon recruited away by a businessman into the management of a company. Successful, he later bought a firm, which, along with a partner, he built into a profitable multi-million dollar operation.

He soon bought other businesses, real estate, country club memberships, a Mercedes for his wife and a sports car for himself. Life was good for him.

As I met with him over time, his dissatisfaction with his business partner became increasingly apparent. His ill feelings started to dominate our conversations. In spite of all of his outward success, he had become very unhappy.

He became so unhappy that all the perks and status meant less and less to him. He found nothing enjoyable. His inability to function with his business partner consumed him.

He finally sold his interest in the company, but continued his pattern of blaming others for his problems.

He felt that it was "always them" who held him back. Nonetheless, he found himself "swimming in cash," enough so that he could live comfortably off the interest for the rest of his life.

Then he went into another partnership and soon lost hundreds of thousands of dollars. The partnership began to dissolve because of his inability to deal with his new partner. He tried another partnership. That, too, ultimately dissolved, and he eventually started another company. By that time, it was too late. Most of his fortune was gone. Soon, the IRS was after him.

The final step in his downward spiral came when he left and divorced his wife of twenty-six years.

What a great teacher he was. It's never in our best interest to blame another person. We are the only ones responsible for ourselves. Rather than spending time getting our story straight, it is more valuable to search for solutions to the challenges at hand, to close the loop.

Finally, that's what my young friend did.

He drew a line and stopped blaming others for his failures. He remarried, started a new business and appears to be extremely happy and successful. There is never any criticism or ill feeling about the war, the first marriage, the former partnership, nothing. He is always positive, and upbeat, and this is reflected in his success. He chose to change and has become one of the greatest success stories I have ever met.

*To close the loop, let go of your anger*

I love the old story told about the farmer who became angry at the railroad because of the way they handled a "right-of-way" through his property. He was so enraged that one day he told his friend that he was going to do something about it. He was going to buy a ticket on the train and not use it to demonstrate his hatred for the railroad.

Or, as one of my friends put it, "I hated that teacher in high school so much that when I took his course, in order to get even with him, I flunked it."

**Blaming someone else gives you "permission" to fail and evade responsibility for your failure.**

As long as we can lay defeat on someone else's doorstep, we won't feel as guilty about it. When we take control of our own lives and **commit** to our changes, accepting responsibility for what happens to us, we gain enormous power and insight over our present and future.

Perhaps the most significant step in changing is to go from getting your story straight to closing the loop. When our singular objective is to bring whatever endeavor it is that we are facing to completion, to finish mile twenty-six plus the 385 yards, we are in charge of our own lives.

### *When you start to get your story straight, look at the achievements of others and be encouraged*

There will always be a mile twelve, where we are tempted to begin making excuses. One way to close the loop is to look at people who have not let temptation keep them from doing what they set out to do.

**It's better to find people who will bring out the best of what is inside of me than to get my story straight, and make it okay to fail.**

The morning I ran the New York City marathon, I looked through *The New York Times* sports page for

146

information on the marathon. An article about a man with a transplanted heart, who planned to run the marathon, inspired me. Through a chance conversation, he had met the family of the 16-year-old boy who had donated the heart to him. The boy had committed suicide but wanted his organs donated.

When I was tempted to get my story straight during my run, I thought of that heart transplant recipient and his courage brought out the best in me.

I also thought about Fred LaBow, who had died from cancer two years earlier. I ran alongside Fred in his last race, the 1992 New York marathon, which he finished after he was diagnosed with brain cancer. After he finished, he went back to the course everyday for the four days it took a war veteran to complete the marathon. The veteran did not have any legs and propelled himself along on his hands. Fred cheered him on every single day until he closed the loop.

Fred also cheered on a woman suffering from multiple sclerosis, who took over a day to complete the marathon on crutches. Her name is Zoe Koplowitz. I saw Zoe in New York and have a poster in my office where she is leaning on the crutches that she used to run her ninth marathon. If she can do it on crutches, I think, I may be able to do it in perfect health.

## *Failure is an experience, that's all it is*

The strength of our commitment to a successful change stems from our ability to regard failure as a temporary obstacle, and not the end of the game.

**Even if we fail, we can still close the loop.**

Jim, who owns an office machine company known for its excellent service and quality, presented a highly attractive proposal to a large local utility, but lost the bid to a competitor. Jim asked the buyer at the utility why he had lost the order. The buyer was very clear in his response. He told Jim that his proposal was excellent and that his price was even lower than his competitor's, but that he could not remember a week passing without the other company "banging on his door." The contract was eventually awarded not to the company offering the best price or service, but to the firm that was the most persistent. The competitor did not stop, and in time they closed the sale/loop.

*The race does not always go to the swift, but often to the persistent*

Persistence is a state of mind. Even persistent physical effort flows from mental resolve.

When I write, work out, or engage in other activities that require mental discipline, there are times when I *mentally decide* that it is okay to give up. Soon after, I usually do. It's easy to find an excuse to quit. If one is not readily available, it will appear.

When I go running, other runners often ask, "How far today?" I'll answer the number of miles I plan to run that day, be it six, eight, ten or twenty. Doing so locks me into a specific distance. Telling them how far I plan to run means that I have made a commitment, and I know that once I have done that, the task is as good as accomplished.

## A winner is simply someone who does what they say they are going to do.

We can train ourselves to view failure any way we want. Failed attempts are so often regarded as the final statement of fate. However, we can train ourselves to gain abundant wisdom, knowledge and strength from defeat.

*Defeat is an education*

The defeat of the moment – the failed romance, the lost job, the missed opportunity – is often part of the fabric of our future success. It provides the opportunity to develop, to become strong, resilient and observant. It often allows us a chance to reinvent and re-create ourselves. The worse the failure, the greater the opportunity is to rebuild. As a friend said to me, "A setback is a setup for a comeback."

Many people who have had great accomplishments have had to overcome tremendous heartbreaks. They refuse to be discouraged. They often are so goal-oriented that they view obstacles as only temporary hindrances, a nuisance to be overcome. They know that if they keep moving toward their goal, most of the obstacles in their path will fall away.

During the Depression, the then unknown bandleader, Lawrence Welk, had his band quit on him during an engagement in a small South Dakota town. He asked why. "Because of you, that's why. We don't want to spend the rest of our lives out here in the sticks, and that's where you're going to be for the rest of your life. You're never going to make it in the big time. You're still bouncing around like you're playing at a barn dance somewhere, and you can't even speak English very well. You're the one who's holding us all back."

Lawrence Welk called it, "the day the band quit." He was heartbroken, but refused to stop. Of course, Lawrence Welk went on to become one of the most famous entertainers in the world.

There is an interesting "chain reaction" to success. Often, one person's stubborn refusal to allow failure to keep them from closing the loop provides another with energy to close their own loop, whatever it may be. When Anne Sullivan Macy first met Helen Keller, she met a spoiled and erratic child prone to tantrums. Macy had to teach Keller in an era before there were any established methods of communicating with the deaf, mute, or blind. Helen Keller was all three.

To teach Helen Keller to communicate, Macy held Keller's fingers on her nose, lips, and throat, so that Keller could feel how they moved when she spoke. Macy then repeated simple patterns over and over until Keller learned them. It was only through Macy's persistence that Keller learned to communicate at all. Keller went on to graduate from Radcliffe with honors and a degree in English literature. Keller's victory was based on another's refusal to view failure as anything but a temporary setback.

One experience that has stayed with me for many years is what I call, "the day I got the hook."

I had contracted with the local U.S. Coast Guard recruiters to give a two-day seminar. On the first day of the seminar, in front of the forty enlisted recruiters present, I just didn't have "it." I was not performing very well at all.

At the end of that day, the lieutenant in charge told me that he might call that night to cancel the next day's session.

That evening, I went with a friend to hear Charles "Tremendous" Jones speak. He gave an inspiring presentation in which he told of a seminar he gave in Houston in which he was not "tremendous." It was one of the rare days that he simply "bombed."

He said he had been feeling glum, discouraged, dismayed, and thought, "Maybe I should try another line of work." When he had arrived back at his hotel room, a postcard from his son who was away at college awaited him. He and his son tried to communicate every day, usually with postcards. He said that he had been  so uplifted by the card, that he totally disregarded the failure his presentation had been. It helped him put things in perspective.

When I got home at 10:30 that night, the message of my cancellation was waiting on my voicemail. It was the first time I had been cancelled in over twenty years in the business. While I didn't need the money that badly, my ego was bruised. I hadn't measured up. It was an "earthquake" for me.

But then I thought of Charles "Tremendous" Jones and his poor performance in Houston. I realized that if it could happen to one of the giants of the business, then it certainly could happen to me. I love that old line in our work: "There are only two kinds of people: those that have bombed and those that are going to bomb again."

Perhaps the most dramatic instance I know of closing the loop is embodied in the example of Evanghelos Georgakakis. In 1944, Georgakakis, a Greek soldier, stepped on a German land mine. The mine exploded, blinding him, obliterating his right hand, and leaving his left hand useless except for one finger. Upon his return from the war, Georgakakis was barred from high school. He took a job assembling brooms and brushes with his teeth.

*We are capable of amazing feats, if we persist*

Georgakakis eventually got into high school by demonstrating he could read Braille – with his tongue. Before he finished high school, he applied to law school and was admitted.

In May 1966, twenty-two years after Georgakakis stepped on the German mine, the people of Athens were amazed when a blind man without hands came in first out of 360 candidates in the bar exam.

## *Summary*

Keeping our stories straight keeps us blocked to the possibility of positive change and growth.

Our commitment to changing begins with accepting responsibility for whatever happens in our lives.

Blaming someone else gives you "permission" to fail and evade responsibility for your failure.

It's better to find people who will bring out the best of what is inside of me than to get my story straight, and make it okay to fail.

A winner is simply someone who does what they say they are going to do.

Even if we fail, we can still close the loop.

# Stage Eight: Recycling

This stage can occur at any point in the above process. It's natural to cycle and recycle through some of the stages. Many of our journeys through change chart a complex course. For example:

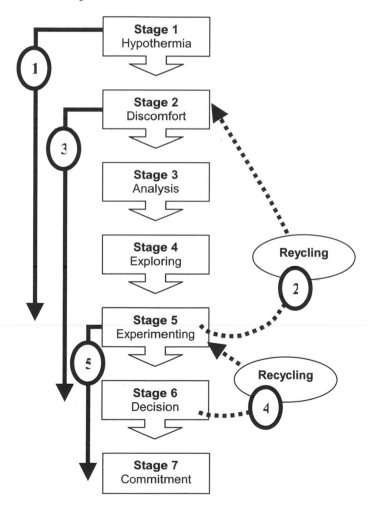

### Change is a continuous process

Just as our bodies might reject an organ transplant, our lives might reject a change. It is natural that we shut down the system and reject a change or become indifferent to it. This is our way of coping.

Some may call this stage a *relapse*, which has negative connotations with "falling off the wagon." It is actually a valuable and necessary – if exasperating – stage of change. The important thing is pressing forward through each stage.

Also, because nothing stays the same for very long, even if we have moved through all the stages of change and created a wonderful new situation for ourselves, it is to be expected that at some point, life will call upon us to go through this cycle again.

When we decide to make a change, we sometimes push back against it and try to figure out ways to revert to the way we were. This resistance is often subconscious.

Our bodies will sometimes fight against organ transplants – even though they could save our lives. we do the same when traumatic change happens. We shut down the system, make ourselves ill, become clinically depressed.

The solution? *Accept what we cannot change.* If we can accept the inevitable and seek whatever professional help that is available to work our way through what has occurred, we can **recycle** through our stages of change.

Sometimes, even when we seem to be successful, we need to begin the process of change all over again.

I was working with a young client, in his early thirties, who had been a jet pilot in the Navy during the Vietnam War. I asked him if he had been in combat and he said no, he had become a flight instructor. I asked him how he accomplished that.

He told me that when he graduated number one in his class, he realized that if he became an instructor, he would not have to land his jet on a heaving carrier deck in the dark, at night, off Vietnam. He said, "My mama didn't raise no fools." Being shot at over the jungles in Vietnam and landing on a carrier deck at night, or becoming a flight instructor in Florida; it was an easy decision for him to make.

He said his time in the Navy was the most exciting, wonderful and fulfilling time in his life. So then the question was, if he had been so successful in a thrilling career, why had he resigned?

"There are an enormous number of managers who have retired on the job."

**Peter Drucker**
Management consultant

He answered, "I was no longer growing, and when you are no longer growing, you are dying."

I realized this young man was telling me a story of **recycling**. He reached the **Commitment** stage (stage 7), where he was able to finish first in his class, choose his own career path, and enjoy success. Then, quite naturally, after time, the jet pilot recycled back into the **Hypothermia** stage (stage 1), where he was no longer growing, or learning.

Even flying a jet, it seems, can become mundane.

**Recycling** is a necessary and natural part of the change process. It's how we "take our temperature" – figure out where we are, where we have come, and where we're going. It's how we rejuvenate and begin the process again.

As we recycle through changes, we should keep in mind habits and ways of thinking that can make us less than effective. These habits can hamper us at any stage of a process of change. They include our reactions to *stress*, our *attitude*, whether of not we *compound* our problems, how we deal with *perceived adversity,* how we *empathize* with others, and the way we *use our energy.*

### Minimizing stress

The best advice I have heard about dealing with stress came from a New York City cab driver, of all people. As we sat stalled in rush hour traffic, horns honking and tempers flaring, the driver cheerfully edged the cab over to the curb, put two wheels up onto the sidewalk, and traveled a block like this until we were able to turn down an empty side street, avoiding the traffic mess. Although the area was filled with honking and cursing New Yorkers, my driver optimistically whistled a tune and virtually beamed a ray of sunshine throughout his cab.

I told the cab driver how impressed I was. I said he seemed the happiest, most enthusiastic, and positive man I had met in New York or in any place in a long time.

He told me that he had been driving a cab for ten years. I asked him if he had always been so cheerful. He replied, "No, I drove a bus for thirty-eight years in New York City until I finally couldn't take it any longer. I developed an ulcer and I quit."

I asked him, "Was that from fighting all the people in New York?"

"No," he replied, "it was just from fighting myself. When I starting driving cabs, I stopped wrestling with my inner demons. I decided no matter what happened, if I couldn't change it, I would just 'flow with it.' My ulcer disappeared and my life has been an absolute joy ever since. I just stopped fighting myself."

Instead of looking inward – like the cab driver – and asking how we might be causing ourselves undue stress, we often look to reduce stress though other means.

We might self-medicate through the use of alcohol, tobacco, junk food, caffeine and recreational, prescription or over-the-counter drugs. All of these practices are unhealthy for both the body and the mind.

But there are some forms of stress relief accessible to virtually all of us throughout our day-to-day lives.

Exercise rids us of a lot of tension in a very healthy way. The physical exertion of exercise supplies more oxygen to the brain, which stimulates the release of chemicals that benefit our state of mind. Our brain, then, is a natural pharmacy providing us with the prescriptions we need to run smoothly and efficiently.

Another excellent means of reducing the chance of burnout, although not as common as exercise, is to *talk* out the issues that are causing us stress. Psychotherapy is often called the "talking therapy," because it is founded on the observation that simply talking about our problems reduces stress and increases our ability to cope. Discussing our situation with a professional has, in the past, been seen as a sign of an unbalanced individual. In reality, it is one of the most natural methods of releasing tension and avoiding burnout.

Something I learned through personal experience to be very helpful in dealing with stress or change is *doing something for others.*

For eighteen years, we had a beautiful black cocker spaniel that originally belonged to our son. When Jon left home, the cocker spaniel and I became the best of friends, and I considered him to be the most devoted, loving, friendly and gentle dog I have ever had the good fortune of knowing. Finally, much to our dismay, he became so sick that it became clear that his eighteenth year would be his last. One day, when his pain became too great to continue, I took him to the vet and made the necessary arrangements. Sitting in my car after leaving him with the vet, I gently wept.

Change had come in the form of something I could not challenge. There was nothing more to do. I was depressed.

I went to my office to prepare for the balance of my workday, yet I could only sit quietly at my desk, immersed in the grief and pain of loss. I keenly felt the loss through death of many people in my life I have loved very deeply: two brothers, two sisters-in-law, my mother, my father, and two sets of aunts and uncles who were instrumental in my formative years.

Something prompted me to call a close friend of mine, a man whose sister was working in a mission in Alaska helping and supporting unmarried, native mothers-to-be. My friend gave me her phone number and I called and spoke with her. I encouraged her in her efforts and arranged some financial support for her mission.

*Helping others can help us deal with our own pain*

After speaking with her, I could almost immediately feel the pain subsiding and the depression lifting. I began to look at the recent loss of my beloved dog in a different light, and felt truly grateful for the eighteen years that we were blessed with his presence.

Getting outside of myself and focusing on helping someone else completely relieved this absorption with self and my loss.

## Choosing your role models

A powerful way to gain courage when we are recycling through the stages of change is to look at the lives of those we respect and admire. The common thread I've found in many people who have become prosperous and successful is that they have been heavily influenced by at least one other individual. This person can be almost anyone: a parent, author, scoutmaster, schoolmate, teacher, minister, an aunt, uncle, or a neighbor.

I believe we naturally, even unconsciously, select people in our lives as role models. I've been fortunate to have a number of role models in my life. Some are famous people I've only encountered briefly or not at all. Others are people I've known or worked with.

Harold Nilsen, who was two years older and a grade ahead of me was a role model in elementary school. The fact that Harold was a great athlete and "worldly" before it was cool to be worldly probably improved his status in my eyes. He was the only person I had ever seen play baseball skillfully without a mitt, fielding the ball better with his bare hands than most people do with a glove. Harold's teams usually won as a result of his batting and fielding skills. At sixteen, he dropped out of school to become a merchant seaman, his career for the next forty years.

I went through a phase during which I wanted to be just like him, traveling the world as a seaman. Harold Nilsen became a *picture* for me, but only for a short time. I changed and chose not to follow in his footsteps.

Another of my idols, Norman Vincent Peale, is quite well known. Of all the books I read at the start of my career in human development, his classic, *The Power of Positive Thinking*, had the greatest influence on me. The way Dr. Peale conducted his life and career as a writer, speaker and teacher became a model for my life.

Years later, when I had established my own career as a public speaker, I was standing in a ticket line at the Cleveland, Ohio airport. I realized the man standing in front of me with a briefcase in his hand looked like my hero, Norman Vincent Peale. I had seen him on TV, so I knew what he looked like. I noticed that his briefcase had a gold-stamped monogram: "NVP," and became certain it was him.

Excited, I wanted to talk to him, to tell him how much I had enjoyed his work, and how much he had influenced my life. I had been on the road for two weeks and was eager for human contact.

As I started around his left side to introduce myself, he turned his back and blocked me off. Gently, I moved to his right side, and he blocked me on that side as well. He could sense that I had recognized him and moved to discourage contact.

Unable to get him to acknowledge me, I ended up not saying a word to him. As I flew to Detroit that night, I thought about how I regretted his actions. Maybe he was weary or had different things on his mind or just didn't want to talk.

Thinking about it, I realized he was still a fine role model for me. I decided to *take the best and leave the rest.*

Many years later, I had an opportunity to introduce Dr. Peale at a breakfast meeting. In our conversation that day, I didn't mention that night in the Cleveland airport.

When Dr. Peale got up to speak, he was very dynamic for a man in his eighties, clear and enthusiastic. He had a wonderful message. However, I noticed at times that he was also somewhat acerbic and strident in his views, more than the situation warranted. While he was positive, he chose not to smile that morning, and in a couple of examples, he took a somewhat critical tone.

*Take the best and leave the rest*

I realized that when I modeled myself after him, I would choose to emulate his enthusiasm, clarity and diction, and forget about his other cryptic and unnecessarily pointed comments.

Another person I chose to study and emulate was Don Bennett, with whom I was in business for seventeen years. Don was one of the most charming, effective, and empathic people I had ever known.

Don Bennett taught me how to express gratitude; he showed me how to listen, and how to understand another person's point of view. Most importantly, he taught me how to sell. Don also introduced me to skiing and taught me about being devoted to children. I learned values and habits from Don that helped me to focus on other people.

Warren Buffet is another person on the list of people I choose to model myself after. Not because he is one of the richest men in the world, but because he is the best in the world in his chosen field. I'm impressed at his ability to study and stay focused, and to become so proficient at predicting the stock market. When I see him on TV and read his writing, I am struck by both his style and his wit. I respect people who enjoy success and are strong but kind; confident but not overbearing; gracious but not smarmy, and who demonstrate humility.

Following Warren Buffet's example, I choose to lead a life that will enable me to achieve for as long as I live.

I often reflect on a 16-year-old wrestler I saw who competed even though his legs had been amputated above the knees. He was outstanding as a wrestler. He said, "I never see myself as handicapped, I never see myself as disadvantaged."

We can find people to emulate and inspire us continually. Who we select is our choice. We can choose people who are bogged down with their own ailments or troubles, or we can choose people who have overcome the obstacles in their paths.

When I was becoming a charter boat captain, I had two role models. One was an older Norwegian fisherman who ran his own 42-foot trawler out of Westport, Washington. Jon and I spent many evenings with him. He had fished off the coasts of Alaska and Washington for fifty years. He knew where the fish were, he knew the water, and he knew his boat. I often wondered what it was like to be as skilled and competent as he was.

My other role model was a charter boat captain. The boat he operated always returned first, with limits for all his charters. On his boat, he was an effective manager and a successful executive. More than anything, he was a consummate gentleman, always considerate of his passengers.

*Models help us see the steps we need to take to achieve success*

Once I understood that I could be like these two men, learn what they knew, and execute like they did, my goal became possible. I pictured myself like them. I emulated the way they held themselves, the way they conducted themselves, and how they performed. I had to

161

*visualize* myself as a successful charter boat captain in my mind before I could become one in reality.

**The best way to succeed at what we choose is to study what those who have gone before us have done and learn from them the steps they have taken.**

The purpose behind finding a model is not to *imitate*, because then we will become only a mirror reflection. The purpose is to *emulate*. We study the picture of the other person's life and achievements, learn from it, and become our own unique person.

When we are recycling through stages of change, referring to our role models can be a tremendous help to the process.

### *Your attitude is your choice*

Much of life is *attitude*. If we can learn to accept the unchangeable and not focus our concern on the circumstances of our life that we have no control over, we become more efficient in handling the things we *can* control.

We take one thing at a time, balance work and play, and maintain our support system through interaction and involvement with others. We then can more readily accept the challenges that the stress of change presents to us.

**No one has control of your mental attitude except you.**

This is beautifully illustrated in an article written by Chase Patterson Kimball, M.D. entitled, "A Predictive

Study of Adjustment to Cardiac Surgery" (*The Journal of Thoracic and Cardiovascular Surgery*).

The study involved four different groupings of patients who suffered from heart disease and were required to undergo cardiovascular or open-heart surgery.

Group One was described as *Adjusted*. They were reality-oriented and purposeful. They coped well with stress. Even though they were quite ill, they continued to successfully conduct business and domestic affairs. They viewed the impending surgery as desirable and necessary. They could express uneasiness, fear and anxiety about the surgery, but they were in control of these emotions. They acknowledged that death was a possibility, but they were basically optimistic that the operation would be a success.

Group Two was labeled as *Symbiotic*. This group had adapted to their illness to the point where they were achieving gains by being sick. They had considerable dependence on a parent or spouse or caregiver, and they received tremendous attention as a result of their condition. Their cardiac symptoms were often precipitated by feelings of being threatened. This group approached surgery with a view of maintaining the status quo.

Group Three was described as *Denying Anxiety*. The symptoms and signs of their illness were denied or minimized. They did manifest uneasiness about the surgery, but they couldn't verbalize their fears. Instead they appeared rigid, hyper alert, suspicious, and hyperactive. Many were sleepless and had no appetite. Their relationships with the hospital staff were stilted, and they were unable to talk about death.

Group Four was categorized as *Depressed*. They gave varying accounts of how they had coped with stressful events. Some relayed sagas of life-long disappointments and hardships. Others had successful lives but had experienced deterioration in their ability to

163

cope with the onset of their cardiac symptoms. Common among the members of this group was that they all had given up in their efforts to live with their disease. Their outlook on surgery was one of hopelessness, and they believed that the medical procedure would be of "no use," and that they could do nothing to affect the result.

*Your attitude can be the difference between life and death*

The eventual outcome of the study was just what we might expect, knowing what we do about how attitude affects our ability to deal with stressful events.

The *Adjusted* group included thirteen patients. Nine improved in health, three remained more or less unchanged, and one died because of a mechanical mishap.

The *Symbiotic* group included fifteen patients. One died, while one improved. The rest remained unchanged or got worse.

The *Denying Anxiety* group included twelve patients. Four died, three of them during surgery. Three improved, three remained unchanged, and two became worse.

The *Depressed* group included fifteen patients. Eighty percent of this group, eleven patients, died.

### Don't compound the negative

For centuries, individuals and doctors have attributed accidents and illnesses to bad luck, carelessness, acts of God, even the weather.

**We must all make an effort to shed the comforting notions that assign responsibility elsewhere, and understand that we are as much to blame for our circumstances as is any outside influence.**

I saw a perfect example of this in a friend of mine who was afflicted with cancer. In my visits with him, he told to me that his son had recently lost a very difficult custody battle in which the son's wife sued him for divorce, and after a protracted and agonizing legal battle, she had won sole custody of their young son, my friend's grandson. My friend told me that soon after the court's decision was handed down, his son took the child and disappeared, leaving behind a note proclaiming that he would not return for the next eighteen years.

My friend was extremely distraught over this and explained to me that within months of his son's and grandson's disappearance, he was diagnosed with the cancer that was now destroying him. He also told me that he had discussed in great length with his doctor and another professional whether there was a direct relationship between his illness and these events. He concluded that yes, there was a connection.

Within a year of telling me of these events, my friend was dead.

My friend's reaction to the changes in his life *compounded* his problems. In addition to having to cope with his son and grandson's disappearance, he also had to deal with the ravages of cancer. By his own conclusion, if the bitter custody battle had never occurred, resulting in his losses, he likely would not have had cancer. I stress, *his* opinion.

If we can control our responses to sudden and forceful changes we wish had not happened, we can avoid compounding our problems.

### Perceived adversity

Often, we place stress on ourselves, by regarding events in our lives as unfair or negative when, in fact, they are marvelous learning experiences and the outcome could be very positive. This is *perceived adversity*.

A few years ago, I served on a board of directors in New York City with a man who bore the same name as a very large, very successful, high profile investment banking firm on Wall Street. He told one of the more fascinating stories about perceived adversity.

It seems that when he was young, in high school and college and soon thereafter, he was a very colorful and spirited young man. In fact, by the time he graduated from college, he was, in his words, already a "full-blown alcoholic." His family, fearing that he would squander the vast fortune left in trust for him, took legal action to keep the funds from him until he showed that he would not abuse them.

Years later, after becoming sober and showing that he was prepared to manage his inheritance responsibly, he received his entire fortune intact. His siblings, meanwhile, having received their trust funds years earlier, weren't as fortunate as their newly rehabilitated brother. They had, through poor investments, some dissipation and poor management, lost much of the money they had received from the family fortune.

*Sometimes, bad luck is not so unlucky after all*

The storyteller would laugh uproariously as he relayed the notion that the most negative, demeaning circumstance of his life turned out to be, perhaps, the most fortuitous.

He went on to have a very successful career and experienced high achievements in the treatment of alcoholism, even founding a nationally recognized treatment facility.

What had seemed a hardship turned into a stroke of good fortune.

## *Empathy: the key to changing attitude*

Empathy is the ability to understand other people's feelings and see things from their point of view. It is appreciating that how others see and feel is based on their experiences and their needs.

Over the years, I have come to believe that the ability to relate to other people and understand their feelings, and why they react the way they do, is one of the most important factors in successful human relations.

A long-time friend of mine, Chris Hegarty, told me a story that illuminates how empathy can change one's opinion.

A mother took her three-year-old son Christmas shopping for the first time. The mother was excited about taking her son downtown to see all of the lights, the decorations, displays, and to visit Santa Claus. She was sure her son would love the excitement of the Christmas shopping experience as much as she had as a child.

After about fifteen minutes of walking from store to store downtown, the boy told his mother that he was tired and wanted to go home. The mother couldn't understand and was a little aggravated that he wanted to go home so soon. After the third time the boy asked to go home, she glanced down and noticed that his shoe was untied.

As she bent down to tie his shoe, she was now at his eye level, and she realized why her son was so uncomfortable. Instead of viewing the decorations and elaborate displays, she found herself looking at the underside of the sales counter, which was stuck with a piece of old gum. The floor underneath the counter was not carpeted but covered with dirt and water that people had tracked in from the snow outside. People and their packages bumped her as they walked by.

Seeing the world through someone else's eyes can be a great gift

From that viewpoint, she realized that it was not a pleasurable experience for someone two feet tall, and she took her son home to wait for the opportunity to return with her husband so that they could take turns carrying him.

Often, it takes only a minute to view matters from a different perspective, but many people don't make the effort. When we take the time to examine a situation from more than one angle, we often find that other people have valid reasons to have different opinions than we do. When we understand the concerns of others from their point of view, it helps us to solve problems more constructively.

If we fail to see things from someone else's viewpoint, we may take actions that others find offensive. We may do things that have a negative impact on our businesses, careers and relationships.

**In most cases, we take actions that have negative impacts on our lives because we fail to see important situations from any perspective other than our own.**

A lack of empathy can harm the careers of otherwise very capable people.

I worked with a man running for the Washington State legislature. In all of my years, I have never met anyone more intelligent or physically stronger. He was generous and giving with friends and a great father and husband.

But in long discussions with him, I found that he refused to see how other people saw his "act." He could not empathize, and it cost him.

The first year he ran, his party enjoyed tremendous success across the country. Not only did they win on the national level, they won almost every state and local election in our part of the world as well. However, in spite of his party's overall success, this candidate did not succeed in riding the coattails. He was soundly defeated.

As a volunteer and unpaid consultant, I suggested he avoid the inflammatory rhetoric, dogma and personal bias that were so prevalent in his speeches. I asked him to share his views in a more logical, pragmatic and gentle manner.

I discovered he couldn't imagine how he sounded to the people in his audience. He had strong opinions on most issues, but he lacked the ability to understand that the way he expressed himself was insensitive to his audiences and alienated some.

This man and I also belonged to an organization. I was fascinated to see that he raised more money than anyone in its eighty-year history, even contributing large sums of his own money. And yet, he also found fault with the way some parts of the organization were run, and mounted personal attacks against other members, without thinking how unconstructive and hurtful he was being. Undoubtedly his intentions were good, but his lack of empathy prevented him from seeing that his fellow members felt his actions mitigated all his previous good work in the organization. They came to feel that his giving had been an aberration!

He failed to gain the recognition and acceptance he sought through politics and his charitable work because of his inability to feel empathy for others.

When we initiate change, we are empathizing when we identify how the change affects those around us. When we are caught in the middle of change initiated by someone else, we are empathizing when we identify how the people undergoing change feel and why they are making these choices.

**If we want others to like, love, and respect us more, we have to respect and honor everyone in our environment, even those who are hard to love.**

I'm often asked by business owners and managers what they should tell an employee who asks, "How well am I relating to other people in the company?" Should they tell the team member about negative feedback that they have heard from peers and supervisors?

I have concluded that we owe it to the people who ask us to gently but clearly tell them if their "act isn't selling." By telling them that their behaviors annoy or anger others – if we tell them in a clear, dispassionate, straightforward manner without intent to hurt – we give them a *chance to change*. If they don't know, they certainly won't change.

## Because your energy is finite, use it to enrich your life

So much of what we do to fight change saps our energy. I liken this to an experience we had with an electric stove in our kitchen.

*Use your energy wisely*

One day, I noticed that the stove was not heating properly. It took a long time for the top burners to get warm and they didn't have the red glow that electric stovetops have when they are sufficiently energized. The oven also took much longer to heat and did not reach the set temperature.

An appliance repair firm came to fix the stove and suggested that we should begin by checking with our electric utility to ensure that the house was receiving sufficient energy. We asked the electric utility to check it out, and they discovered that the main electrical cable leading into the house had been resting on a rock. Apparently, the current running through the cable caused it to vibrate and rub against the rock, which in turn, wore out the insulation surrounding the electrically charged wires. The repairman explained that the house was not, in fact, receiving the required amount of electricity; some of if was wastefully flowing directly into the ground around the break in the cable.

This is what happens when we *misdirect* our energy and allow anger and resentment to steal its flow.

**When we waste our energy on things we cannot change, flailing against the inevitable, we rob ourselves of the energy that is needed for every other aspect of our lives.**

This energy can be saved and used to create, to love, and to do the productive things that we need to do to achieve our dreams and objectives. In youth, our energy seems inexhaustible; but, as we have other demands and responsibilities placed on us, we recognize that our energy has limits – it's finite.

### We each have the ability to become a "change master"

I started this book with the story of my friend Ralph Palmerbeing shot. Consider his situation: he was lying in a hospital bed, recuperating from the emotional trauma of a gunshot and the physical invasion of surgery, performed in an emergency situation. His resources were low.

Many people in his situation would be tempted to funnel their energy into anger at their faceless attackers, who remained at large. For some, such an event as getting shot could signal a complete downhill slide; they would allow their reaction to compound the stress and its effects, leading to possible recovery complications, such as some of the heart patients in the study mentioned earlier. They would always have a "story that would sell," a built-in excuse to fail that anyone would buy.

However, Ralph took another path.

Instead of wasting his precious resources dwelling in anger, blaming others, and feeling victimized, he decided to find something positive about the experience. After some effort, he had the idea that his surgery might improve his golf game. And he was right – his game *did* improve!

Ralph efficiently used his energy to move rapidly through the stages of change and get on with his life in a positive, effective way.

Every one of us has this choice. When we have the tools and the knowledge to confront change, we learn how to accept whatever happens and find opportunities where before there appeared to be none.

You have the power to guide yourself through the stages of change. When you realize that change is a process and you have tools to manage it, you have great power.

**Every day, all of us have the opportunity to turn change into a payday – it's our choice.**

### *Summary*

No one has control of your mental attitude except you.

We must all make an effort to shed the comforting notions that assign responsibility elsewhere, and understand that we are as much to blame for our circumstances as is any outside influence.

In most cases, we take actions that have negative impacts on our lives because we fail to see important situations from any perspective other than our own.

If we want others to like, love, and respect us more, we have to respect and honor everyone in our environment, even those who are hard to love.

When we waste our energy on things we cannot change, flailing against the inevitable, we rob ourselves of the energy that is needed for every other aspect of our lives.

Every day, all of us have the opportunity to turn change into a payday – it's our choice.

# Suggested Reading

The following books are among the best of many that have shaped my views regarding change, determination, and vision.

**Cadillac Desert: The American West and Its Disappearing Water** by Mark Reisner (Penguin Books, 1986)

**The Carolina Way: Leadership Lessons from a Life in Coaching** by Dean Smith and Gerald D. Bell with John Kilgo (Penguin Press, 2004)

**8 Critical Lifetime Decisions: Choices That Will Affect the Quality of Your Life** by Ralph Palmen (Beacon Hill Press, 2001)

**Feel the Fear and Do It Anyway** by Susan Jeffers (Fawcett Books, 1988)

**Good to Great: Why Some Companies Make the Leap and Others Don't** by Jim Collins (HarperBusiness, Harper Collins, 2001)

**Man's Search For Meaning** by Viktor E. Frankl (Pocket; Revised and Updated edition; 1997)

**The Power of Positive Thinking** by Norman Vincent Peale (Ballantine Books; Reissue edition, 1996)

**Seabiscuit** by Laura Hillenbrand (Ballantine Books; 2001)

**Undaunted Courage: Meriwether Lewis, Thomas Jefferson, and the Opening of the American West** by Stephen E. Ambrose (Simon and Schuster, 1996)

# Index